CHANGING THE WAY WE DO CHURCH

8 STEPS TO A PURPOSEFUL REFORMATION
2ND EDITION

JOHN W. STANKO

urbanpress

Changing the Way We Do Church, 2nd Edition
by John W. Stanko
Copyright ©2020 John W. Stanko

ISBN 978-1-63360-149-9

For Worldwide Distribution
Printed in the U.S.A.

Urban Press
P.O. Box 8881
Pittsburgh, PA 15221-0881
412.646.2780
www.urbanpress.us

To retired Pastor Rock Dillaman, the elders, pastors, staff, and members at Allegheny Center Alliance Church on the North Side of Pittsburgh, PA. Thank you for welcoming me to the ACAC family back in 2001. It was an honor to serve with you on staff from 2009-2014 and to still be part of the ACAC church family today. I pray that together we will continue to learn and then do church the way God wants it to be done. To God be the glory!

TABLE OF CONTENTS

INTRODUCTION

One of the advantages of getting older is that one has more experience. One of the disadvantages of getting older is that one has more experience. I am getting older as I revise this book which I first wrote when I was 59 years old. Now I am 70. I have been involved in church work for just short of 50 years and I have seen a lot of things—the good, the bad, and the ugly, you might say. That is both a help and hindrance as I continue my church work and re-write this book.

Being older is a help because I can more readily connect and compare what I observe now to things in the past and I have more past experiences which I can relate to the present. My experience allows me to make effective assessments and decisions more quickly. When I speak, people tend to listen, willing to give me the benefit of the doubt that I just may know what I am talking about. *After all*, they think, *he is older so he must be wiser.*

Getting older is a hindrance, however, because one begins to think, "I have seen it all. I have seen this and it's bad (or good)." Because I have been through more, I can be more cynical, distrusting, impatient, and guarded. I have never talked to anyone who has worked in a church setting and did not at some point have something happen to them that was hurtful, even devastating. When I was young, I could afford to be idealistic. Now that I am older, I don't have time to waste pursuing long-term possibilities. I am much more interested in reality.

Yet if we are going to discuss the Church and what it will take to reform it, which is what I will discuss in this book, then we must talk in ideals, for the ideal is the vision and model from which we build and work on a daily basis. I was born in 1950, so I was raised on idealism. As a college student in the '60s and '70s, I was part of the generation that wanted to reform government, education, and any other institution we could get our hands on. Then I met the Lord in 1973 and transferred my focus for reform to the Church, reacting to "established religion," seeking rather to break off and build what we called "New Testament" churches that would more accurately reflect what we saw in the book of Acts.

The experiment with those New Testament churches has been a rougher ride than expected. We thought if we sat around a circle, holding hands and singing our favorite chorus, all would be well. It was not. We knew we inhabited earthen vessels, but we underestimated just how earthen we were. At the same time, we overestimated the Spirit's willingness to overrule just how "earthy" we are. Therefore, some things happened that our idealism said would never happen, things like sexual abuse, betrayal, financial mismanagement, and nepotism. When they did, many of God's soldiers went missing in action or joined the army of the Church's enemies.

We experienced the pain of aborted community as people who joined together in one accord were only too ready to separate shortly thereafter, sometimes over trivial matters (and at other times over more serious ones). We had to endure the ignominy of scandal after public scandal as pastors, televangelists, and other leaders showed that our idealism and trust in them had been misplaced. Today, I know many who have decided to sit the "church thing" out and just worship God in the safety of solitude, or the relative anonymity of churches that do not emphasize community.

In 2001, my world came crumbling down when I left a church and a man with whom I had been associated for 27 years. It was painful. I have not and will not go into the details in this book or in any other publication. Suffice it to say the transition from that situation tested me to the core of my being.

I was tested in the values I held and taught like missions, giving to a church, and even church attendance. My idealism was shipwrecked and marooned and I didn't know if I wanted it back.

Yet through it all, I can say my wife and I never missed attending a Sunday service in a local church after our transition, even though we came in limping and bleeding. We passed the test and in 2009 I found myself back on a church staff as an administrative pastor with an emphasis on disciple-making, which ended (well, I might add) in 2014. I've come a long way, but in some sense, I am right back where I started in 1973— with a strong commitment to the local church and its role in extending the kingdom of God on earth.

When my world ended, so to speak, in 2001, I had to start over in ministry, building new relationships and finding my voice—the message I had to deliver without rancor or bitterness. Since I had lost everything and everyone, I began to dabble in technology without being a "techie." All I understood then and now is where the on button is on my tech toys and tools, so let's just say my learning curve was steep. When I wrote the first edition in 2009, I did not even think to include a section on technology, for my confidence in that realm was still limited. I felt like the least likely candidate to lecture the body of Christ on how to use social media, which was only a few years old back them.

My commitment to the Church and the Kingdom has led me to write this book, titled *Changing the Way We Do Church: Seven Steps to a Purposeful Reformation* (this revised version will add an eighth step). I am writing precisely because I am older and I have seen a lot. Yet I still believe Jesus gave His life to build the Church so I cannot offer anything less. I write this book because I have been an elder, part of the Church's "board of directors" for many years, and I share responsibility for her failures. I must therefore take a role in building her future, as disqualified and inadequate in some respects as I feel I am to do so.

The Seven Steps (now joined by an eighth step) I presented in the first edition are the result of traveling four million miles since 1989 visiting churches and ministries across the United States and around the world. I write having served as an associate pastor, home or cell group leader, senior pastor, administrative pastor, executive pastor, itinerate speaker, director of a nonprofit (NGO, for my non-American readers), college professor, author, and church member since 1973. I have served as a church consultant and am certified to administer the Natural Church Development church profile, which I have done for 50 churches. I have served on numerous governing boards and have heard thousands of sermons, some good and some not so good. I have preached with the same results from time to time.

I earned one doctorate from an unaccredited institution and corrected that mistake by earning a doctor of ministry degree from Reformed Presbyterian Theological Seminary in Pittsburgh in 2011. I have read or listened to hundreds of books that cover a variety of topics and authors from quantum physics to the Dali Lama (although I still don't understand what he is talking about; I guess I am not enlightened). I spent a total of four years overseas from 2001 to 2009, mostly in Africa, so my conclusions and suggestions are not only based on American experience. Believe me when I write that idealism where the church is concerned and failure to live up to those ideals are not American phenomena.

I have pioneered a message on purpose and have written extensively on that topic, while conducting 3,500 purpose interviews and coaching sessions since 2001 (I know because I kept careful records). I have seen firsthand how powerful the purpose message can be. Much of what I write will emphasize various aspects of purpose and how they can contribute to a much-needed church reformation movement. With amazement and pain, I have watched great leaders and ministries self-destruct by failing in one or more of the "big three"—sex, money, and power. Surprisingly, the "power failure" has been more prevalent than the other two, sex and money, in my experience.

I will chronicle my technology and social media credentials in the new section of this book that addresses those two entities. I have done a lot in that area since 2009, and really began in 2001, taking some baby steps that have led me to where I am today. As I write, I sit in my home office and send out messages, videos, broadcasts, books, and classes from my desk and those media reach people all over the world. When the COVID-19 pandemic hit in 2020, I didn't miss a beat because I was prepared to use all the means at my disposal to continue my purpose work. More on that in the new section.

I am not bragging when I tell you where I have been and what I have done. I am just reminiscing in part for my own good, trying to talk myself into re-writing this book. Plus, I do not want you to accept what I present just because I wrote them, but I don't want you to dismiss them out of hand either. They are the result of a lot of thought, prayer, successes, and mistakes, even if they seem misguided or off the mark in your estimation.

Let me say that I have no church in mind when I write this book. I have been in enough churches to compile one story from many sources. The stories I include are real, but they are often a composite of multiple church situations so no one example is drawn from one church scenario. The names have been changed to protect the guilty and sometimes I was the guilty leader in the examples used.

It is an accurate statement that the Eight Steps I recommend all stem from the reality that there is a leadership crisis in the modern Church. A number of years ago, I wrote a book entitled, *So Many Leaders, So Little Leadership*. The message in that book is more applicable today than it was when I wrote it. There is a price to become and then to be an effective leader of God's work. It requires a different mindset and we will study some of the biblical leadership directives as we go along in this book. If the eight steps are to be taken, it will be by a radically new leadership from what we currently experience in the Church.

I have found that many determine at the outset to be good leaders or better leaders than what they had previously experienced. The problem is that they have determined to be better leaders in a bad system with a flawed paradigm for what a leader is and does. The answer is not to be a kinder, gentler leader but to be a radically different leader that our God expects—and Scripture demands. The times require nothing less.

There is the old saying that if you want what you have always had, then keep doing what you have always done. If we want to see something different in the Church, then we must do something other than what we are doing. I present these Eight Steps in the hopes of contributing to the leadership dialog that is raging right now on the Internet and in church circles and seminaries. I also know, based on my experience, that applying any (if not all) of these Eight Steps will bring your church closer to the biblical model we read about and study in the New Testament. Applying them to your own life will produce nothing short of a personal revival.

Let me add that when I say "church" or "Church," I do so with the realization that there are many churches and expressions of churches in the world today. I would categorize them by their worship mode as either liturgical or Word-based—churches following a set order of service with little preaching and teaching or churches that have a set order that usually culminates in a lengthy lesson taken from the Bible. The labels Catholic or Protestant don't really work for there are some Protestant churches that tend to be more liturgical, although there are no Catholic churches that are Word-based.

My world has been the non-liturgical evangelical churches so that is what I am addressing in this book. I do believe that liturgical churches can and should draw on the Eight Steps as often as possible, for it is the liturgical churches that are experiencing the greatest crisis at this time.

Let me say three more things as I close this introduction and begin the book. I was on staff at Allegheny Center Alliance Church (ACAC) in Pittsburgh when I wrote the first edition. These Seven Steps were developed and taught long before I joined the staff, so this book is not a statement about or to my friends there. I applied some of what I present in my position at ACAC and will share some of the results I saw during my tenure.

Second, I have included, at my first publisher's suggestion (this second edition is published through my own company), a set of discussion questions at the end of each chapter. I have included questions you can ask about yourself, and questions that would be good for small group discussion with friends or colleagues. If your church is serious about embracing one or any of the Eight Steps, then these questions will guide you through the process.

I conclude the second section with Chapter Eleven where I describe three simple steps that any church can apply now that will enhance their ability to be more purposeful and embrace the spirit of the Eight Steps at the same time. The new third section on technology begins with Chapter 12, along with more questions to help you think through and hopefully apply the concepts I present. Then I wrap up with a few additions in the Appendix where I further explain the concepts of increase, self-promotion, permission marketing, and what I call the metrics of discipleship.

Finally, I hope you will feel free to write me with your comments and suggestions that will strengthen and enhance what I write in *Changing the Way We Do Church*. My contact information is included at the end of this book, and I look forward to engaging you on the reformation journey. The work of reformation is hard and it's not pretty, but it is a team effort and I hope this book inspires you to join me in reforming the Church of Jesus to become what He intends it to be.

John W. Stanko
Pittsburgh, PA USA
April 2009 (first edition)
September 2020 (second edition)

SECTION ONE

A NEW LEADERSHIP

SINNERS IN THE HANDS OF AN ANGRY LEADER

More than a few years ago, I visited a large church to meet with the staff at a colleague's recommendation. The objective was to give the pastor there some feedback and recommendations concerning his staff's strengths and weaknesses after my colleague informed me that the church was in crisis. What I found when I got there was somewhat surprising, but all too typical.

After profiling the staff and making some public presentations, I began to meet one-on-one, first with the pastor and then with each staff member. During those meetings, I discovered a lot of mistrust, anger, and fear. Although the church had every appearance of success—large facilities, multiple services, multifaceted programs—a great deal of dissatisfaction and even dissension was in its midst.

I made my report to the pastor after two days, and his response was one of anger bordering on fury. He said, "There aren't any problems here, especially with me or my leadership style. The problem is the staff. They are lazy. I am giving them names of people, and they aren't following up to build this church. The answer is not for me to understand their different personalities and styles, as you suggest. The answer is that I should fire every last one of them."

I was paid for my time (a check commensurate with what the pastor thought of my services), thanked for the visit, and dismissed a day earlier than I had planned. What happened as I walked to my car, however, was even more revealing. Many of the staff thanked me for coming as I was walking out the door to my car. One man said, "You're one of the few who has ever spoken honestly to him [the pastor]. He can be so mean, and the church is being run by a few of his favorites."

Another commented, "We need what you've done. We're going to do all that we can to get you back here as soon as possible!" One more said, "This is the first time I can re- member open and honest communication taking place among the staff." But I left, knowing I would never be invited back to that church—and I wasn't.

For the Eight Steps of church reformation I outline in this book to be applied, we must see them as tools to address the depth of the leadership crisis in the Church and society today. We will also need to face the fact that servant leadership is sorely lacking in most places—even in the Church. We know how to talk and preach about love and service to others and we have loads of books on leadership, but we don't know how to combine the two into one concept called servant leadership.

According to most reports I see, church attendance continues to dwindle, and the pandemic of 2020 is not going to provide relief from that trend. We complain the Church cannot compete with modern trends that make church service like attending a baseball game—long and monotonous. Instead of working to make services more relevant or energetic, some leaders have chosen to double down on what they have always done while relying on and hoping for a spiritual revival that will enthuse and inspire people to return to the pews. I fear we are waiting and praying for something that will never happen or for something that can only happen if we make some changes and transform, which I call a reformation.

AUTHORITATIVE STYLE VERSUS SERVANT-LEADERSHIP

My life's work and passion are to help people find their purpose. If people are to find their purpose, they will need leaders who know how to focus on the people and not people who focus on the leaders. If people are to fulfill their purpose, they will need leaders who take seriously the job description for the ministries of the apostle, prophet, evangelist, teacher, and pastor:

> It was he who gave some to be apostles, some to be prophets, some to be evangelists, and some to be pastors and teachers, *to prepare God's people for works of service, so that the body of Christ may be built up* until we all reach unity in the faith and in the knowledge of the Son of God and become mature, attaining to the whole measure of the fullness of Christ (Ephesians 4:11-13, emphasis added).

I want to help leaders understand how destructive an angry, heavy-handed style can be to both themselves and the people they lead. I want people who are experiencing this form of abuse to realize that this is not God's endorsed style of leadership. I want those who are called but not yet in leadership positions to formulate a gentler, Christ-like leadership philosophy, becoming servant leaders in the process.

This problem, however, isn't restricted to the Church. Recent business scandals, bank failures, and bonus payouts for bogus results show that authoritarian leadership is alive and well in the corporate world. Government failures across the world also point to the leadership failures of elected officials. Voter turnout rates indicate many voters have opted out of the democratic process.

For the sake of this discussion, however, we will limit our focus to the Church, knowing that lessons need to be learned by all who are leaders, both in and out of the Church. If the Church reforms and produces godly leaders, those leaders can and will find their way into every walk of life. Wouldn't that lead to a healthy societal transformation?

In the context of the Church, we often find one strong man or woman, usually the founder or someone related to the founder, who has built the church through a mix of gifts and personality. Sometimes we find an authoritarian board that controls the pastor and much of what goes on in the church. This leader or board exercises authoritarian leadership styles reminiscent of Moses or the Old Testament prophets. And that is the problem: Because this style is sometimes depicted in the Bible, it is assumed that it is godly. It is not.

In reality, Moses and the prophets were servant leaders. They influenced rather than controlled, and they had to trust the Lord for their leadership results. It was written of Moses, "Now Moses was a very humble man, more humble than anyone else on the face of the earth" (Numbers 12:3). The King James Version renders the word *humble* as *meek*. This indicates someone can be a strong, effective leader who deals with the things of God without being authoritarian.

The problem with an authoritarian style is that, while it may be useful to build a church to a certain size, it isn't effective in managing the church once it tries to grow beyond that size. What's more, that style tends to "chew up" people who are trying to serve the vision of the leader.

ANGER AND THE AUTHORITATIVE STYLE

I have found the dominant characteristic of this

leadership style is anger, and thus I have entitled this chapter, "Sinners in the Hands of an Angry Leader." You may recognize the title is a variation of Jonathan Edward's famous eighteenth century sermon, "Sinners in the Hands of an Angry God." I have observed an abundance of anger among church leaders in general. Their anger has injured many whose life purpose, gifts, and experience have been lost or severely hampered as they tried to serve the church.

The Bible is full of examples of authoritarian leaders and in each case, anger characterized their leadership style and relationships with their management teams, followers, and associates. Let's quickly look at a few of these leaders:

1. **Moses**. Moses was a product of his age, and authoritarianism was the rule of the day. While Moses was meek and a great leader, it is interesting that his anger prevented him from entering the Promised Land, the goal of his leadership. His anger caused him to misrepresent the Lord when he was dealing with the people. After the Lord had told him to speak to the rock to bring forth water, we read in Numbers 20:11, "Then Moses raised his arm and struck the rock twice with his staff. Water gushed out, and the community and their livestock drank." God honored Moses' leadership by providing water, but Moses was not permitted to enter the Land. His problem: anger.

2. **King Saul**. As Saul got older, his anger became more pronounced. His trusted number-two man, David, had great success in battle, and the people honored him for his achievements. Saul did not share in the people's joy: "Saul was very angry; this refrain galled him. 'They have credited David with tens of thousands,' he thought, 'but me with only thousands. What more can he get but the kingdom?' And from that time Saul kept a jealous eye on David" (1 Samuel 18:8-9). The Bible tells us Saul tried to assassinate David on three occasions and spent much of his latter reign pursuing David in order to eliminate his heir to the throne.

3. **Herod the Great**. Herod ruled during the time of Jesus' birth. History tells us he arranged to have family members and rivals to the throne murdered, and then spent the rest of his life mourning them. When the Magi who came to visit Jesus did not follow his instructions, "he [Herod] was furious and he gave orders to kill all the boys in Bethlehem and its vicinity who were two years old and under" (Matthew 2:16).

4. **Jesus' disciples, James and John.** During one trip, the Samaritans prevented Jesus and His disciples from passing through their territory. "When the disciples James and John saw this, they asked, 'Lord, do you want us to call fire down from heaven to destroy them?' But Jesus turned and rebuked them" (Luke 9:54-55). Jesus wasn't impressed with the men's appeal to what I call an Old Testament persona. Some leaders feel obligated to express a stern style since they believe it is how God wants them to be. Jesus rebuked His followers then for their anger and thoughts of revenge; He would do the same today.

5. **The Sanhedrin and the High Priest.** These Jewish religious leaders enjoyed their position of authority, and they were angered when anyone challenged them. That is one of the reasons they killed Jesus. They were jealous of His popularity and angry the people wanted to follow Him. This anger is also seen in the death of Stephen, the first martyr. "When they [the Sanhedrin] heard this, they were furious and gnashed their teeth at him . . . At this they covered their ears and, yelling at the top of their voices, they all rushed him, dragged him out of the city and began to stone him" (Acts 7:54, 57).

You can see from these leaders that anger was their trademark. Their anger fueled jealousy, fear, intimidation, and even ruthless tactics. Authoritarian leaders have little patience for those who do not respond quickly to their demands. They see themselves as owners and not stewards and take most dissent as a personal affront requiring swift retaliation, lest the dissension spread like a virus and their vulnerability be exposed.

The problem, of course, is that most followers are imperfect. It is just a matter of time before those imperfect followers stir up the wrath of the authoritarian leader, thus the title, "Sinners in the Hands of an Angry Leader." Let's examine one more biblical character and that is Elisha, the great Old Testament prophet.

6. **Elisha, the great Old Testament prophet.** He raised the dead, performed some unusual miracles (like causing a metal axe head to float on water), and delivered the word of the Lord to God's people. Working with Elisha was difficult, however, because he had a temper. Historically, his temper has been excused, overlooked, and even justified because he was a "prophet of the Lord." The common assumption is that the deaths he caused were the will of God in response to the sins of those who died.

I want to challenge the supposition that it was God's will for those people to die. What if Elisha's anger, coupled with his prophetic power, somehow released a curse on the people he was supposed to bless? What if the Bible, by reporting Elisha's actions, wasn't endorsing them but simply reporting them as historical facts? Let's look at the three examples to which I am referring:

- **2 Kings 2:24-25:** Forty-two youths were mauled because they mocked the prophet of God. Was that God's will, or did Elisha's anger unleash a harsh sentence on some irresponsible youth?

- **2 Kings 5:23-27:** Gehazi was wrong to pursue Naaman and take a contribution his master had already rejected. Was the just sentence for his folly a lifetime of leprosy for him and his family?

- **2 Kings 6:32-7:2:** On the one hand, the king had sent a group to kill Elisha, and he simply had the door barred with no punishment for the king's behavior. On the other hand, an officer asked how such a seemingly impossible prediction of immediate, bountiful supplies could be possible, and he paid with his life. When I ask modern prophets why this officer deserved death, some tell me he died due to his lack of faith in the prophet's word. Is unbelief a worse crime than murder? Why was the king spared and the officer sentenced to death? There is a possibility that Elisha's anger was the cause. I see a pattern of anger in Elisha's life that made it difficult to be around him when he was challenged or questioned. Do you see this as possible? Or do you consider this the Old Testament prophetic syndrome mentioned earlier?

As a leader (and a strong one, I've been told), I've had to deal with, and am *still* learning to deal with anger. I have reflected again and again on the words of James, who wrote, "Everyone should be quick to listen, slow to speak and slow to become angry" (James 1:19). He didn't say never to be angry; he cautioned that anger should not be immediate. I'm not implying a leader should never be angry; what I am suggesting is that anger should not be the predominant emotion in anyone's leadership style, especially someone who is committed to become a servant leader.

I can't change anyone's leadership style. Only the Holy Spirit can do that. I can, however, allow the Spirit to change *my* style, and that involves confronting my own anger. I want the fruit of the Spirit—love, joy, peace, patience, kindness, goodness, faithfulness, gentleness, and self-control—to be a central part of my leadership style. I want to be a good listener and learn to talk a lot less.

DEALING WITH ANGER

Perhaps you have suffered firsthand, as an imperfect person, at the hands of an angry leader. I encourage you to forgive and then allow those lessons to impact your own leadership style. You have a choice to replicate that anger or to eliminate it from your own style of management. I trust you will choose the latter and become a leader who is relatively free from anger as you guide God's people—or even people in the marketplace who may not serve or know the Lord. Remember, David learned more from King Saul than from anyone else about leadership—he learned how *not* to lead! You can learn a lot from a poor leader, but only if you replace the bad with the good.

Perhaps you are a leader who was or is angry. People have felt the sting of your anger, and perhaps they were wrong in what they did—but that doesn't justify your anger. You must repent and ask their forgiveness. You need a new heart to lead or else your anger will cost you the Promised Land as it did Moses. You cannot apply the Eight Steps that I am about to outline if you are angry. It just won't work.

To help you be the leader God wants you to be, I direct you to three simple principles found in Peter's first epistle:

> Be shepherds of God's flock that is under your care, serving as overseers—not because you must, but because you are willing, as God wants you to be; not greedy for money, but eager to serve; not lording it over those entrusted to you, but being examples to the flock (1 Peter 5:2-3).

How can you avoid the angry leader mentality? These verses give three helpful tips for any leader who wants to be more effective. First of all, *lead willingly*. Some leaders are angry with the people because they are angry with God. They don't want to lead or at least don't want to engage the personal development required to be effective. Second, *lead without focusing on money.* Third, *lead as a servant,* not as an overlord. The last two speak for themselves and are clear.

It's a new day that requires a more open leadership style in the Church and society in general. If we want what we have never had, we must do what we have never done, and that certainly goes for leadership styles and the expected results. If the Eight Steps in this book are to be successfully implemented, we must see the old anger/authoritarian style put aside and new paradigms for servant leaders applied to existing and future leaders.

CHAPTER 1
QUESTIONS FOR DISCUSSION OR STUDY

1. Have you ever experienced an angry leader? What do you remember about that encounter? How did it make you feel?

2. If you are a leader, what makes you angry? Do you express that anger? Do you think your anger has injured anyone? Do you need to go and make amends?

3. How do you think you can guard against leadership anger, either your own or anger coming from another person?

4. The time to decide what kind of leader to be is when you aren't leading. Then you can establish your values and not be affected by money or power. What is your leadership philosophy? What kind of leader do you want to be, by God's grace?

5. If you are already leading, what steps can you take now to reduce your anger and change your leadership style? One step is to redefine and clarify your values, especially in the way you view and treat people.

6. David learned how to lead from Saul by watching how not to lead. Who are your leadership models? What did you

learn from them? Is there anything you need to un-learn from them? Do you need some new models? Where will you find them?

7. Go back and read 1 Peter 5:2-5. Meditate on these verses regularly. What did you learn? How can you incorporate what you learned into your leadership style?

8. Read Luke 9:51-56. What can you learn about anger in ministry from that passage? How did Jesus address the subject?

SERVANT LEADERSHIP IS THE ANTIDOTE

The only cure for the leadership crisis is an entirely new style of leadership along with an entirely new concept of follower. Let me point out at the outset of this chapter that I am not anti-leadership. While I appeal for a more inclusive, less authoritarian style of leadership, I am not dismissing the importance of leadership in the overall scheme of the Church or society.

Effective leadership was what brought the great reforms to the Church over the centuries. Great leaders were the ones who withstood the onslaught of heresy and pioneered new movements and insights into worship, church structure, and theology. Godly leadership was what led to the civil rights breakthroughs in my own nation, and leadership brought down the apartheid system in South Africa. People of faith have brought great change and innovation to the fields of medicine (Florence Nightingale), social justice (Sojourner Truth), and commerce (Cyrus McCormick), just to name a few.

14

Leaders, however, cannot do all the work of the ministry or their chosen domain of work, and they must stop trying. They must be people who know how to include others in the work and who follow the model of the apostles in Acts 6 when they gave responsibility to the people to care for the widows because they weren't about to step away from that they did best. More on that later.

Yet the greatest leaders are those who know how to use their power to further their cause and empower others. Leaders cannot empower anyone if they don't have the power to do so, so power isn't a bad thing per se. It is when that power turns selfish to build a monument or to promote the leader, however, that things often go horribly wrong—or fall far short of what could have been accomplished.

THE POWER OF SERVANT LEADERSHIP

In 1998, I read Robert Greenleaf's collection of essays titled *The Power of Servant Leadership*. That book took my breath away as I was confronted about my own faulty leadership style. I wept and agonized over what I read for days, as I asked myself, *Why have I never heard about this in the Church? Why didn't I ever preach or speak about this myself?* I determined from that point forward not only to study and teach about servant leadership, but also to embody and model its principles. I saw that servant leadership was the antidote and cure for authoritarianism or weak, ineffective leadership.

As I did, I found that while my new style was pleasant for the people and followers, it was hard on my fellow leaders. I have had more than one leader and pastor tell me, "You can't allow people to do what they want. You have to tell them what to do. Otherwise, you won't build the Church [or business]." I had another pastor tell me, "The purpose message won't work. It gives people too much freedom." I had still another tell me, "I don't want that message in my church. I have everything set the way I want it, but if the people hear you, they will all become free agents and abandon what I have them doing."

In a sense, what they said is true. Leaders must direct and guide the people, or what's the use of leading? In a larger and more important sense, however, they were wrong. Their mistake is the problem with leadership that will keep the Eight Steps I am about to present from ever being tried and applied.

When I was in Indonesia many years ago, I was teaching servant leadership to a group of bank executives. One of them raised his hand and asked, "Didn't Jesus teach about servant leadership?" I thought that was an interesting question from a man in the largest Muslim country in the world. He knew that servant leadership was part of Jesus' message. Why doesn't the Church know?

In Luke 22, we find Jesus' explanation and summary of servant leadership. Jesus was gathered in the upper room with His disciples for what is now known as the Last Supper.

> Also a dispute arose among them as to which of them was considered to be greatest. Jesus said to them, "The kings of the Gentiles lord it over them; and those who exercise authority over them call themselves Benefactors. But you are not to be like that. **Instead, the greatest among you should be like the youngest, and the one who rules like the one who serves.** For who is greater, the one who is at the table or the one who serves? Is it not the one who is at the table? But I am among you as one who serves" (Luke 22:24-27, emphasis added).

This wasn't the first time Jesus had this discussion about service with His followers. But, as He prepared for His death, He found it necessary to review it one more time because they were arguing over who had the most significant ministry. He then went on to practice what He preached by giving His life for those same followers.

Service isn't easy, but it's what leaders and pastors must do if their leadership is to be mature and effective. It requires humility and a firm grasp on purpose and values. Leaders who serve followers have found the way to prevent power from corrupting their leadership. They've also found that the way to keep from manipulating and controlling followers is through the simple mindset and subsequent actions of service. Robert Greenleaf wrote,

> The servant-leader is servant first. It begins with the natural feeling that one wants to serve. Then conscious choice brings one to aspire to lead. The best test is this: do those served grow as persons, do they, while being served, become healthier, wiser, freer, more autonomous, more likely themselves to become servants?[1]

The major objection to leaders also being servants is generally rooted in something that sounds like this: "I'm not working for people; they are working for me. I won't and can't have members or employees telling me (leadership) what to do." This reveals a faulty understanding of servant leadership and a bit of insecurity as well. To clarify this misconception, I turn to Ken Blanchard, well-known author of *One-Minute Manager* fame. He explains concerning traditional leadership,

> Most organizations are typically pyramidal in nature. Who is at the top of the organization? The chief executive officer, the chairman, the board of directors [the pastor or board]. Who is at the bottom? All the employees—the people who do the work . . . The paradox is that the pyramid needs to be right side up or upside down depending on the task or role.

> It's absolutely essential that the pyramid stay upright when it comes to vision, mission, values, and setting major goals. Moses did not go up on the mountain

with a committee. People look to leaders for direction, so the traditional hierarchy isn't bad for this aspect of leadership.

Most organizations and managers [and church leaders] get in trouble in the implementation phase of the leadership process. The traditional pyramid is kept alive and well. When that happens, for whom do people think they work? The person above them. The minute you think you work for the person above you for implementation, you are assuming that person—your boss—is *responsible* and your job is being *responsive* to that boss and to his or her whims or wishes. As a result, all the energy in the organization is moving up the hierarchy, away from customers and the frontline folks [or staff and members] who are closest to the action.[2]

Blanchard's remedy is to turn the pyramid upside down for the implementation. He further explains, "That creates a very different environment for implementation. If you work for your people, what is the purpose of being a manager? *To help them accomplish their goals.* Your job is to help them win."[3] That sure sounds like Ephesians 4:11-13 to me.

THE POWER OF A LEADER

There's no question a leader has power. I'm *not* advocating leaders surrender that power, but rather that they use their power in a manner benefiting both those who follow them as well as the organization that everyone, including the leader, is serving. A pastor once stated that authority is like soap: the more you use it, the less you have. Too often, leaders succumb to the temptation to use power to achieve personal goals or to get people to do what they want, regardless of whether the followers have had time to process what that will mean for them or the organization. It's all about the leaders.

I again quote the following passage from the Apostle Peter because it is so important to this discussion. The apostle Peter wrote in his first epistle:

> Be shepherds of God's flock that is under your care, serving as overseers—not because you must, but because you are willing, as God wants you to be; not greedy for money, but eager to serve; **not lording it over those entrusted to you, but being examples to the flock** (1 Peter 5:2-3, emphasis added).

And the apostle Paul wrote in his letter to Philemon this interesting appeal:

> Therefore, although in Christ **I could be bold and order you to do what you ought to do, yet I appeal to you** on the basis of love. I then, as Paul—an old man and now also a prisoner of Christ Jesus—I appeal to you for my son, Onesimus, who became my son while I was in chains. Formerly he was useless to you, but now he has become useful both to you and to me. I am sending him—who is my very heart—back to you. I would have liked to keep him with me so that he could take your place in helping me while I am in chains for the gospel. **But I did not want to do anything without your consent, so that any favor you do will be spontaneous and not forced** (Philemon 8-14, emphasis added).

In each instance, Jesus, Peter, and Paul were addressing people in leadership. They were giving them a different way to lead, one that gave followers room to grow, make decisions, and respond to the will of God and leadership out of a willing heart. These men understood that, as the adage goes, a man convinced against his will is of the same opinion still.

POWERFUL INFLUENCE, NOT POWERFUL CONTROL

The Old Testament includes a story involving the prophet Elijah and his initial contact with his successor, Elisha. It provides an example of a leader influencing followers and not controlling them. Let me set the background for the story.

Elijah was in a bad place. He had run from Jezebel, the queen who wanted to have him killed, and he ended up hiding in a cave. The Lord spoke to him there and asked him why he was hiding. Elijah responded, "I have been very zealous for the Lord God Almighty. The Israelites have rejected your covenant, broken down your altars, and put your prophets to death with the sword" (1 Kings 19:10). Because of these terrible conditions, Elijah was suffering from depression. The Lord "encouraged" him by giving him something to do:

> The Lord said to him, "Go back the way you came, and go to the Desert of Damascus. When you get there, anoint Hazael king over Aram. Also, anoint Jehu son of Nimshi king over Israel, and anoint Elisha son of Shaphat from Abel Meholah to succeed you as prophet" (1 Kings 19:15-16).

That sent Elijah on a mission from God and he set out on his journey to find Elisha, his successor. What did he do? Did he come to Elisha and make a dramatic scene? Did he relate to Elisha all that God had said? Let's look at what he did.

> So Elijah went from there and found Elisha son of Shaphat. He was plowing with twelve yoke of oxen, and he himself was driving the twelfth pair. Elijah went up to him and threw his cloak around him. Elisha then left his oxen and ran after Elijah. "Let me kiss my father and mother good-by," he said, "and then I will come with you." "Go back," Elijah replied. "What have I done to you?" (1 Kings 19:19-20).

This story impresses me every time I read it. Elijah, armed with "the word of the Lord," didn't use that word to hit Elisha over the head. He just *touched* him with it, leaving room for Elisha to determine on his own what had happened and what his response was to be. I interpret this to be an example of a leader using influence but not control over someone who was to be a follower.

Servant leadership does not mean the leaders become a doormat, as many have expressed that concern. Servant leaders don't have to tiptoe around their peers or followers. They can be honest and direct with people. Servant-leaders can and should reprimand poor performers and even release them from employment. Servant leaders can be visionaries and set standards, insisting those standards be met. How do I know this to be true? I know because Jesus did it, and He is the model for anyone working in Church leadership—or any leadership for that matter. The giants of industry are not our models. Jesus is and He was an effective servant leader. Even a Muslim knows that.

Elijah "touched" Elisha and then walked away. We know that because Elisha had to *run* after him once he had been touched. Obviously, Elisha sensed some spiritual significance in that touch, for he went home, closed out his affairs there, and joined Elijah. As far as we know, Elijah never told him to do all that.

More often than not, I've found that if I give followers room to respond to a decision and the will of God, they'll do so positively and in a mature manner. If they don't, then there may be a need to sit down privately with them for further dialogue and communication. If there are two parties in a larger group that get "cross ways," it's sometimes necessary to adjourn the meeting and meet with those two. I've been able to resolve most conflicts in that manner. All the while, however, I'm using my power to influence and not manipulate or control people.

THE IMPORTANCE OF DIALOGUE

Dialogue is an important tool for any leader who wants to influence and not control. Greenleaf commented on this when he wrote:

> Every man is a potential adversary, even those whom we love. Only through dialogue are we saved from this enmity toward one another. Dialogue is to love what blood is to the body. When the flow of blood stops, the body dies. When dialogue stops, love dies and resentment is born. But dialogue can restore a dead relationship. Indeed, this is the miracle of dialogue—it can bring a relationship into being, and it can restore again a relationship that has died. There is only one qualification to these claims for dialogue. It must be mutual and perceived from both sides, and the parties must pursue it relentlessly.[4]

I've found there are a lot of creativity and innovation among followers. When I cut off dialogue or communication or don't give them a chance to speak, even if they are mistaken or simply venting their frustration, then I may lose the creativity or perspective that follower has. Sometimes followers clam up and don't say anything because they are afraid or don't want to dishonor the leader in any way. While that is a good thing to a point, it can obviously be carried to extremes. Reformation leaders cannot allow that to happen.

Ken Blanchard talks of the insight he picked up from a seeing-eye dog training school. He found that schools eliminate two types of dogs: The first group is understandable—dogs that are totally disobedient. But the second group that is disqualified is more of a surprise—dogs that are totally obedient! Schools want to train dogs that follow commands that make sense. If the master commands the dog to step off the curb and the dog sees a car approaching, that dog is trained *not* to obey.

We want and need followers who will stop us from walking out in front of "oncoming cars" we can't see. To have this kind of follower, I must redirect some of my power as a leader to include them in the decision-making process and submit to their decisions when they are functioning in their area of expertise or anointing. I must promote dialogue wherever and whenever possible and appropriate.

PERSUASION VERSUS MANIPULATION

Greenleaf developed the best concept of leaders who correctly use influence I have found. Consider this passage from the book, *On Becoming a Servant Leader*:

> *Persuasion* involves arriving at a feeling of rightness about a belief or action through one's own intuitive sense. One takes an intuitive step, from the closest approximation to certainty that can be reached by conscious logic (which is sometimes not very close) to the state in which one may say with conviction, "This is where I stand!" The act of persuasion, thus defined, would help order logic and favor the intuitive step. But the person being persuaded must take that intuitive step alone, untrammeled by coercive or manipulative stratagems of any kind. Persuasion, on a critical issue, is a difficult, time-consuming process. It demands one of the most exacting of human skills.[5]

The latter statement explains why it's so difficult (especially for people dealing with God's things) to work at influence and not succumb to control—it takes time! Very often, visionary leaders see something so clearly that in their minds it already exists. They therefore feel they must get everyone on board as quickly as possible, and that can lead to well-intentioned but manipulative tactics. The fact that they didn't intend it to be that way doesn't make it any less manipulative.

Greenleaf defines manipulation as "the process of guiding people into beliefs or actions that they do not fully understand and that may or may not be good for them." He goes on to explain:

> Because they are recognized as being better than most at leading, showing the way, they [leaders] are apt to be highly intuitive. Thus leaders themselves, in their conscious rationalities, may not fully understand why they choose a given path. Yet our culture requires that leaders produce plausible, convincing explanations for the directions they take. Once in a while, they can simply say, "I have a hunch that this is what we ought to do." However, most of the time, rational justifications are demanded, and part of the successful leader's skill is inventing these rationalizations. They are necessary, but they are also useful because they permit, after the fact, the test of conscious logic that "makes sense" to both leaders and followers. But the understanding by the follower, if he or she is not to be manipulated, is not necessarily contained in this rationalization that makes sense. Because we live in a world that pretends a higher validity to conscious rational thinking in human affairs than is warranted by the facts of our existence, and because many sensitive people "know" this, manipulation hangs as a cloud over the relationship between leader and led almost everywhere.[6]

BUILDING CONSENSUS

Most leaders find dealing with this "cloud," as Greenleaf calls it, difficult. No matter what business they're in, they are challenged to be patient and allow their followers to work through issues just as the leader did. The answer for Greenleaf is consensus, which is a method of using persuasion (influence) in groups. Four skills are necessary for any leader who wants to build consensus so followers feel some sense of ownership in a decision. They are:

1. The leader must be able to articulate the issues or problem. Patience is required for those who are slower to grasp the situation.

2. The leader must be a good listener. By being a sounding board, the leader sets an example others will follow in listening to all points of view.

3. The leader must be sensitive to the discussions and begin to use his or her power to steer the group to a solution or conclusion.

4. The leader may have to meet with one or more followers who are maintaining a firm position that seems to be against the general consensus of the group. Several options are available, which include deciding not to decide, waiting, or using power to break the logjam and resolve the issue at hand.

I acknowledge this style of consensus building, influencing, and persuasive leadership doesn't work in every situation. In a crisis, strong, experienced leaders are needed to exercise decisiveness as they steer the group or organization out of trouble. Even in that situation, however, there's generally more room for communication, input, and dialogue than is currently utilized in leadership circles.

If you are a leader, or on your way to becoming one, I urge you to consider the content of this chapter carefully. Commit yourself to be a man or woman of influence who is committed to build people up and not tear them down. Be a leader committed to both the vision and the people who are also committed to the vision and take every opportunity to communicate and listen. If the Eight Steps are going to have a chance to work, leaders and pastors must take the role of servants and abandon the role of lords and masters. Without that change, the Eight Steps I am about to unveil will never have a chance to live and flourish. What's more, people at all levels must step forward to accept and fulfill their purpose without expecting the Church to do that for them.

CHAPTER 2
QUESTIONS FOR DISCUSSION OR STUDY

1. Read Luke 22 in its entirety. What was the setting for Jesus' lesson on leadership? What did Jesus say? How can a leader act like "the youngest" (v. 26) and still be an effective leader? Is that possible in your opinion?

2. What can you learn about leadership from the relationship between Elijah and Elisha? Do you see how Elijah left room for Elisha to determine the will of God for himself? How can you effectively employ this practice in your own leadership work?

3. Consider Jesus' interaction with people and His disciples in Matthew 16:13-20, Mark 3:20-30, and Matthew 20:20-28. Notice how accessible He was and how free people were to speak their mind to Him. Where can you model your leadership style after Him?

4. Notice from the passages listed in number three above that Jesus turned every opportunity, including when He was questioned and insulted, into a time for training and teaching. How often do you do the same? How are you doing it? Do you have a website, a blog, a podcast, or a regular time for questions and answers? When you become a leader, what will you do to emulate this aspect of Jesus' life and ministry?

5. How important is dialogue and consensus building when you are dealing with the things of God? Is there room for such activities? Did Jesus engage in these actions? Go back

and look at Matthew 16:13-20. What happened in John 6:1-14? Did Jesus draw out His disciples or just do what He was going to do without them?

6. What about what follows in the rest of John 6? What leadership lessons are there for you in that account? Jesus did not pursue popularity yet sacrificed popularity in order to lead some to the truth. He also submitted Himself to the criticism and questions from the crowd.

SECTION TWO

THE SEVEN STEPS TO PURPOSEFUL REFORMATION

WE WANT
GOD TO "MOVE"

I have been on staff at four churches and worked with hundreds of others as a consultant. I have concluded that we as church members and leaders should eat change for breakfast, so to speak, for we are the Spirit-led people. In the Old Testament, when the cloud moved, the people moved. Sometimes they camped for a day and sometimes for months, depending on how long the cloud had them stay in one place:

> Then the cloud covered the Tent of Meeting, and the glory of the Lord filled the tabernacle. Moses could not enter the Tent of Meeting because the cloud had settled upon it, and the glory of the Lord filled the tabernacle. In all the travels of the Israelites, whenever the cloud lifted from above the tabernacle, they would set out; but if the cloud did not lift, they did not set out—until the day it lifted. So the cloud of the Lord was over the tabernacle by day,

and fire was in the cloud by night, in the sight of all the house of Israel during all their travels (Exodus 40:34-38).

There was never a guidance problem in the wilderness. The people knew what they were to do, and they followed. The cloud protected them from the intense heat of the desert in which they traveled. They could not say to the cloud "You go on ahead. We'll catch up later." They followed the cloud, or they died. It was that simple and straightforward.

We know now that what happened in the Old Testament was for our instruction. Much of it was a shadow or type of what was to come in Christ. Paul mentioned the wilderness cloud when he wrote to the Corinthians, and we should see the cloud as our own standard of how God will move and work with us:

> For I do not want you to be ignorant of the fact, brothers, that our forefathers were all under the cloud and that they all passed through the sea. They were all baptized into Moses in the cloud and in the sea. They all ate the same spiritual food and drank the same spiritual drink; for they drank from the spiritual rock that accompanied them, and that rock was Christ. Nevertheless, God was not pleased with most of them; their bodies were scattered over the desert (1 Corinthians 10:1-5)

Paul showed us it is possible to enjoy every spiritual blessing available but still be displeasing to the Lord just as the Jews were displeasing in the desert. Like the Jews, the Corinthians had all the spiritual gifts and God's presence with them, but they were on the verge of displeasing God when Paul wrote them. We are just as susceptible of falling into the same trap. We are glad to receive the blessings; we aren't always as excited or motivated to follow the cloud. We are glad to *do* church; we just don't want to *be* church. We want God to move; we don't always want to move with Him.

When I speak, I often ask for a show of hands of how many people would like to see God move. Usually almost all hands are raised. Yet if I were to ask those same people, including the church leaders, when was the last time they went through a major change or transition, most would probably indicate it has been a while. They would probably even recount the way that change was forced on them by a job loss, death of someone close, or some other "act of God."

Usually when people want God to move, they want His movement restricted to the public service on Sunday morning or Wednesday evening. They want four hours of church squeezed into a one- or two-hour meeting. They want that time to be unscripted and filled with the unexpected. Yet then they want to go home and have life pretty much as it has been—working in the same place, living in the same house, following the same daily schedule until they come back again in one week's time to hopefully have God move again.

I preached a Christmas message one year and used that to point out what it means when God moves. Consider how the people in the Christmas story were affected when God moved as explained by Matthew and Luke. When God shows up, things are put into motion, especially His people:

1. Elizabeth became pregnant late in life after the angel visited her.

2. Her unbelieving husband, Zechariah, could not speak for nine months until the baby was born.

3. When the baby was born, they surprised everyone by naming the boy John.

4. While Elizabeth was pregnant, her cousin Mary also had an angelic visitor announcing she was pregnant with the Holy Child Jesus.

5. Mary immediately went off to pay a visit to see Elizabeth.

6. After Mary went back home, she and Joseph had to go to Bethlehem to register for the Roman census.

7. While they were there, the baby was born.

8. Angels came to unsuspecting shepherds at work, who stopped what they were doing to go and see the Child.

9. Meanwhile, men from the East were following a moving star that led them to the house where Jesus was so they could worship Him.

10. Herod was disturbed by the Magi's visit and sent soldiers to Bethlehem to destroy any male babies who could be a rival to his throne.

11. An angel had warned Mary and Joseph that Herod was coming, so they had already left for Egypt.

12. Eventually, an angel would come back to Joseph to tell him the "coast was clear." Herod was dead and they could return home.

13. They did return to Judea but did not feel safe, so they departed and went to Nazareth.

Do you get the idea? When God moves, angels, governments, shepherds, families, wise men, and ordinary men, women, and children move, too. Why is this important to mention as I present the original Seven Steps (the new Eighth Step will be presented in Section Three)?

It is because the Seven Steps I am about to outline will require change. They will involve leaders changing the way they do business, so to speak, and followers changing the way they follow. The Seven Steps will require that some people move out and leave, and some to come home. The Seven Steps will require that every one of God's people accept their personal responsibility, not just to be spectators to what some do, but instead to be active participants in the plan of God.

It will necessitate that we challenge everything we have accepted as normal to see if it can take us to the next level of activity, relevance, mission, and involvement. If anything cannot do that, then it must be discarded or adjusted. (I am not talking about the basic tenets of the faith, of course; those remain the same.) Are you sure you want to read further?

These Seven Steps, when applied, not only have the potential to change the way we do church, but also the way we relate to the Lord. They will change our paradigm that church is not something we do, contrary to this book title, but something we are and something we express with purpose, the ultimate purpose being to extend God's kingdom and government on the earth.

So enough talk or writing, you say? What are these Seven Steps? In random order, they are:

1. Raise up an army of purpose-led men and women who have faith to do the impossible, freed from trying to be who they are not and released to be the fullest, best expression of who God created them to be.

2. Equip people to perform missions (both domestic and foreign), to launch business ventures, and to carry out any other activity their purpose dictates and faith allows.

3. Help leaders be productive in their purpose as they oversee Holy Spirit chaos created by people pursuing and fulfilling their purpose.

4. Help leaders and governing bodies move from attitudes of ownership to attitudes of servant leadership and stewardship.

5. Develop services, Sunday Schools, kid's church, youth meetings, and even committee meetings that people want to attend because they involve a spirit of excellence and the unexpected.

6. Move from fads, copycat programs, and trite and phony rituals, traditions, and doctrines to innovative initiatives in the Spirit of (but exceeding the results of) the early church.

7. Address and meet the needs of the poor, ethnic minorities, and women around the world.

Let's spend some time looking at each one of these steps and then conclude with some further suggestions for church life in the twenty-first century and beyond. Then in Section Three, I will introduce Step Eight which will require quite a lengthy discussion. Finally, we will move on to my concluding thoughts and Appendices. Buckle your seat belts. You are in for a thrilling but challenging ride!

CHAPTER 3
QUESTIONS FOR DISCUSSION OR STUDY

1. What are your first impressions of the Seven Steps? Which one or ones "jump out" at you upon first reading?

2. Do you agree that we as the Church should be comprised of change agents, thus being a change agent itself? Is this change simply to apply to our public meetings or to every aspect of ministry?

3. Have you considered the movement in the Christmas story? Is that kind of movement to be the exception or the rule for those who are following the cloud of God?

4. How easily do you adapt to change? How can you or your church be even more flexible than you are now?

5. Continue to reflect on or discuss change. Where are you most afraid of change? Why do you think that is?

6. When the Holy Spirit came in Acts, change became a way of life for the church. Consider the following passages in the first half of Acts and discuss what they meant to the early church. What implications do those passages have for you? For the modern Church? (Acts 1:10-11, 15-17; 2:42-47; 4:32-36; 6:1-7; 8:1-3; 11:1-18; 13:1-3; 15:12-21, 36-41; and 16:1-5).

7. Do your own study of Acts 17-28 with the purpose of studying change. How did God institute the changes? What was the response of the people involved? What lessons can you learn from these examples?

8. Was this kind of change only taking place in Acts because it was the early church, or do you think this sets a pattern or provides a model for today? Are these simply examples for church change, or for both church and personal change?

GOD HAS AN ARMY

REFORMATION STEP ONE:
RAISE UP AN ARMY OF PURPOSE-LED MEN AND WOMEN WHO HAVE FAITH TO DO THE IMPOSSIBLE, FREED FROM TRYING TO BE WHO THEY ARE NOT AND RELEASED TO BE THE FULLEST, BEST EXPRESSION OF WHO GOD CREATED THEM TO BE.

Let's look at this First Step, one phrase at a time.

a) Raise up an army of purpose-led men and women who have faith to do the impossible . . .

There is an old song that we sang in church many, many years ago that went something like this:

God's got an army
Marching through the land
Deliverance in their soul
and healing in their hands

Everlasting joy and gladness in their heart
And in this army I've got a part

When we sang this song, we would march around acting as if we were soldiers, feeling quite spiritual when we did. The problem was that the army was content to march around in a circle and not go anywhere. We acted like an army, declared ourselves to be an army, talked about fighting like an army, but when all was said and done, we never went anywhere or fought anyone or anything. If we did, it was an accident. Not much has changed since we sang that song forty years ago. I have watched us be content with reading about what the army should do but consistently failing to do it. At some point, we have to change.

I had one pastor describe church as being in a flight simulator. We can climb in and soar to great heights. We can kill Goliath along with David, part the Red Sea with Moses, be among the five thousand whom Jesus fed, and be with John on the isle of Patmos—all in the comfort of a Sunday flight simulator. We can bank hard, fly fast, and make emergency landings, all from the safety of the simulator. When "church" is over, we get out of the simulator, and we are in the exact same place spiritually as when we entered. We can actually go home thinking we were flying. In reality, however, we were not even close. So what's the answer?

PURPOSE

The answer is purpose, both corporate and individual. In 1981, I discovered my life purpose through a failed business opportunity. I was asking—no, I was begging—God to save that business. When I asked, "If You didn't create me to start this business, what did You create me to do?" He answered me, much to my surprise. (I was surprised because I didn't want an answer. I was simply upset He would not save the business.)

For the next ten years, I dabbled with the purpose

message, applying it to my life and teaching it in my small home group and in prison ministry. In 1991, I had a chance to implement a purpose seminar while traveling with a worship team to conduct conferences. I was surprised at how deeply the purpose message touched people, and I have been speaking, writing, meeting, exhorting, and coaching on purpose ever since.

I thought purpose was a nice message that would go alongside many other nice messages. I didn't know how powerful it was or that it would change many lives. Then Rick Warren's book, *The Purpose Driven Life,* came along, and purpose was suddenly front and center on everyone's mind. I happened to be in the right place at the right time, talking about the right topic. Yet while the popularity of Rick's book has lessened, the interest in purpose has only increased. Why? The reasons are pretty simple:

1. Your purpose orders are your instructions from your heavenly headquarters. They are what God wants you to do.

2. God wants you to know your purpose. He will not play with you or hide it from you.

3. God wants you to fulfill your purpose more than you do.

4. You have the answer to some problem in the world. If you don't address it as only you can do, it won't be addressed.

I won't go into all that I could say about purpose, for that information is available in my other books, on my website and blogs, and in my other resource material (the directions for how to access all those are at the end of this book).

My personal purpose is to *create order out of chaos without control.* I never have to go looking for chaos; it always seems to come looking for me. My purpose is short, clear, and easy to understand, and so is yours. If you don't know your purpose, it's because either you haven't asked to know or you have received an answer you don't understand. The greatest barrier to purpose is in your own mind, but that is easily corrected by simply asking the right questions and processing the answers when they come—and the answers always come.

So what does this have to do with the Church and reformation? The answer is that purpose requires a total shift of thinking where church and leadership are concerned. To some extent, purpose takes the focus off the leaders with their vision and puts it on the people. It requires that the church work to equip people to find their purpose and help them strategize ways to fulfill it.

I have often said that if someone's purpose is to be a swim coach, the church doesn't have to build a pool. If God sends nine swimming coaches to the church, however, then leadership has to ask, "God, do You want us to build a pool?" The answer could be yes, and then it doesn't matter if the pool was part of leadership's vision or not. What matters most at that point is that it was a part of God's vision and, after all, He owns the church, having purchased it with His Son's own blood.

We will discuss this issue further in later steps, so let's move on to discuss the other phrases involved in this First Step.

b) . . . freed from trying to be who they are not . . .

Let's look at another passage to understand this part of the First Step:

> Then Saul dressed David in his own tunic. He put a coat of armor on him and a bronze helmet on his head. David fastened on his sword over the tunic and tried walking around, because he was not used to them. "I cannot go in these," he said to Saul, "because I am not used to them." So he took them off.

41

Then he took his staff in his hand, chose five smooth stones from the stream, put them in the pouch of his shepherd's bag and, with his sling in his hand, approached the Philistine (1 Samuel 17:38-40).

When David went out to fight Goliath, King Saul offered David his armor to wear. David tried it on, but Saul was a head taller than the rest of Israel, so it didn't fit. Instead,

David took what worked best for him—a sling and five stones—and went out to meet the giant.

This is an excellent example of a common mistake many make when it comes to purpose. You cannot be like anyone else as you embrace your purpose. You must be yourself. In my experience, however, I have found people are intentionally *trying* to be who they are *not*. Many people have a personal bias against who they are and don't like who they are and are convinced God wants or needs to make massive changes in them *before* He can use them.

Churches not only need to help members discover their purpose, but they must also help them be more comfortable with who they are in general. This is where spiritual gift profiles and other assessments can help people get a better understanding of what they do best. We must help people focus on the gifts they have as opposed to being uptight about the gifts they don't have. I have often used the following quote from Marcus Buckingham and Curt Coffman's book, *First, Break All the Rules:*

They [great managers] recognize that each person is motivated differently, that each person has his own way of thinking and his own style of relating to others. They know that there is a limit to how much remolding they can do to someone. But they don't bemoan these differences and try to grind them down. Instead they *capitalize* on them. They try to help each person become *more* and *more* of who he [or she] already is. Simply put, this is the one insight we heard echoed by tens of thousands of great managers:

People don't change that much.

Don't waste time trying to put in what was left out.

Try to draw out what was left in.

That is hard enough.[7]

David could not be like Saul when he went out to fight Goliath. He had to be himself and do what he did best. While Goliath was dressed like Saul in full battle regalia, David was able to defeat him by being true to the person he was at that time—a simple shepherd. The people in churches today will accomplish their purpose in the same way, by being who God created each one to be—no more but no less. Yet in saying that, it does not mean they won't need more personal development to fight their own purpose battles. They will, but purpose is always their point of reference.

c) . . . released to be the fullest, best expression of who God created them to be.

While churches must work to help people know who they are—their strengths, weaknesses, gifts, and limitations—we must not leave them in that condition. You may think I am being double-minded, suggesting that people become comfortable with who they are but not staying who they are. I assure you I am not.

Once people find their gifts, purpose, strengths, and calling, it is time to go to work. People sometimes rely on God to do what only they can do. I have often said that if you are ignorant and God anoints you to do something, then you have anointed ignorance. You may laugh, but it's true.

If you are a musician, don't you have to study, practice, and take lessons to do what you do or to improve? Don't you also need to perform so you know what it's like to go from the studio to live performance, making your studio rehearsal time more focused and meaningful? If you are a baseball, rugby, or football player, don't you have to work out, increase your strength and skill, and play often so that you know your teammates, along with their tendencies, strengths, and weaknesses?

If people with those gifts and purposes must work at them, then so must you. What's more, the Church should help you. Churches need to sponsor writing seminars, missions trips (more on that later), theological training, business workshops, counseling workshops, and a host of other appropriate training and equipping sessions so people can build their confidence and skill.

At this point, I can hear leaders and pastors say, "That's not my job!" However, I maintain that it is, and the Bible supports me on this. Paul wrote,

> It was he who gave some to be apostles, some to be prophets, some to be evangelists, and some to be pastors and teachers, to prepare God's people for works of service, so that the body of Christ may be built up until we all reach unity in the faith and in the knowledge of the Son of God and become mature, attaining to the whole measure of the fullness of Christ (Ephesians 4:11-13).

Leaders exist to equip the people for work and ministry. The people don't necessarily exist to support the vision of the leaders (more on that later). We must also stop restricting purpose or equipping people for church work only. We must also be ready to equip and train those whose purpose will be fulfilled outside the church.

I am not implying every church must have all the training there is for their members. They simply need to be aware of what is available and where it can be found so leaders can coach and encourage their members to go for more, even if the church must help pay for some of the expense. This of course assumes leadership is aware of what the members are called to do and where they are to do it.

When many people are seeking, preparing for, and fulfilling their purpose, it requires a different kind of leadership, one that doesn't try simply to control and maintain order. It requires a leadership committed to the success of the people, willing to release them to whomever and whatever will help them fulfill their purpose.

CHAPTER 4
QUESTIONS FOR DISCUSSION OR STUDY

1. Do you know your purpose? How specific is your purpose statement? When have you stopped your efforts in a specific area because it was not connected to who God created you to be and do?

2. What is your church doing to help others find their purpose? What are you willing to do to help those purpose seekers?

3. What do you think is a better investment of time and energy: trying to improve a weakness or maximize a strength? Justify your answer.

4. What are you doing to improve your strengths? What more can you do?

5. How do you feel about the church playing a role in raising up a purpose army by providing various training sessions and programs? Is that part of what the church should be doing? Should the church only offer spiritual training, or can you see a place where the church can or should sponsor a variety of training opportunities?

6. Go back and read 1 Samuel 17 in its entirety of how David defeated Goliath. What motivated David? What history did he have that gave him the idea he could defeat Goliath? What did David say to Goliath? Was he bragging or telling the truth?

7. How has the Church acted like Saul and his army? Was the army fighting or going through constant maneuvers? Did the army encourage David? Did the army advance or stay in the same place?

A SPIRITUAL LOTTERY

REFORMATION STEP TWO:
EQUIP PEOPLE TO PERFORM MISSIONS
(BOTH DOMESTIC AND FOREIGN),
TO LAUNCH BUSINESS VENTURES,
AND TO CARRY OUT ANY OTHER ACTIVITY
THEIR PURPOSE DICTATES AND FAITH ALLOWS.

I have seen countless offerings taken in churches over the years. I have visited churches that don't even mention the offering. Others mention it, collect it, and move on as quickly as possible. Some give a little teaching about giving before receiving it. There are others, however, who make the offering an event, trying to maximize every penny given.

Perhaps you have seen these intense offerings on Christian television. In those instances, a strong emphasis is usually placed on some kind of return. I would imagine this method is used time after time because it works.

In a high-pressure offering, for example, people are

sometimes promised that if they give $951 to a ministry or church, they will receive the blessing of wisdom because there are 951 verses in Proverbs. This makes absolutely no sense, but I regularly see scenarios like that play out. What's more, there is usually a time limit given as well. The money must be given in the next hour or the blessing offer in return for cash is rescinded.

People are hoping to get something and get it quickly, looking for a shortcut to glory or success. You can't blame someone when he or she shops for a bargain. I have found, however, that there are no shortcuts or bargains on the way to success, especially where purpose and the will of God are concerned. Some people are hoping against hope that their next gift, or seed offering as some call it, will help them strike it rich and provide big returns. These people are playing what I call the spiritual lottery. There is no such thing, and most who give under those circumstances are gravely disappointed. Many of them, however, try again not long afterward to give another seed gift, hoping that it will make them rich or successful.

Churches and leaders must help the people understand (and they must first understand themselves) that God does not promote or use gifted people with potential. He promotes gifted people who have had their character developed while they are also developing their gifts and purpose.

I wish a shortcut was at my disposal for writing this book. I wish even more that I could find a shortcut to earning a degree or learning a language. Wouldn't it be great if a shortcut was feasible to start a business that involved no risk and yielded huge returns? And how about finding a shortcut through character formation, where one could wake up one morning and be free from anger, lust, or greed?

I travel the world doing what I do first and foremost because of God's grace. Yet my motto has been Paul's as found in 1 Corinthians 15:10 (NAS): "But by the grace of God I am what I am, and His grace toward me did not prove vain; but I labored even more than all of them, yet not I, but the grace of God with me." I have tried to cooperate with God's grace and work diligently. Are you ready to do the same? Now let's return to the question of how churches can help a purpose army be equipped and trained. I already alluded to it in the last chapter; let's go back and pick up that train of thought again.

a) Equip people to perform missions (both domestic and foreign), to launch business ventures. . .

I noted in chapter four that churches should provide all kinds of training opportunities for their members that are also open to the local community. Much training material is readily available today through the Internet. What a church offers should not be random or simply for the sake of having a training session. It should be geared to the needs of the people who are pursuing purpose. Let me give you an example.

I was in a church once speaking on Sunday morning. I stopped in the middle of my message to take an informal poll, something which I had never done before or since. I asked the 300 people present, "How many of you have thought of writing or illustrating a children's book?" To my surprise, about 50 hands went up. I turned to the leadership who were seated on the stage behind me and said, "We need to have a workshop on how to write and illustrate kids' books." The leadership looked at me like I had a horn growing out of my forehead. To the best of my knowledge, that seminar was never held, and my guess is not one of those 50 ever went on to follow up on what was in their heart and mind to do one day.

Why should a church do that, you ask? They should do that because one of those unwritten books could change the world. It could be a source of financial and spiritual blessing for the writer. That unwritten book could lead children to know the Lord at some future time. That book could stimulate a reader's creativity, and their subsequent creative expressions could also touch the world in some way unknown to us on this side of their writing the book.

The church mourns the lives lost every year through abortion. We will never know what the world missed by not having those babies fulfill their purpose in the world. Yet a similar loss is experienced when we don't allow our ideas, gifts, and creativity to come to maturity among the living. Churches are responsible to make sure that doesn't happen. We must protect life, but we must also ensure that life is expressed to its fullest through purpose.

The title of this subsection, however, speaks about missions and business. Some of what people need to learn cannot be grasped in a teaching session. They need to have firsthand experience on the field or in the boardroom. They will have to get their hands dirty and even fail in the short run to be successful in the long run. Where the church can, it must provide meaningful, learning opportunities for people of purpose.

From time to time, I have taught a missions class for interested parties. One of the statements I make in that class is this: "When God wants to speak to you, He often takes you on a trip." *Why is that?* you may wonder. Let me give you one more example. Once I was returning from a trip to Malaysia, and I sat next to a man who was in a full leg cast and in obvious pain. When I asked what happened, he said, "I was in Malaysia to celebrate the fiftieth anniversary of the end of World War II. I forgot where I was, stepped off the curb, and was hit by a car."

You see, in Malaysia they drive on the left side of the road, the opposite of the United States. That's when my missions class statement made even more sense to me. When you are at home, you can perform tasks automatically, without even thinking of how you do them. Brushing your teeth, driving to work, getting the mail—these are all routine acts and events. Yet when you go away to a new place, you are forced to think in detail about the simplest tasks and how you will accomplish them.

When you do, you are more aware and alert (or else you may get hit by a car), and that makes you more open to hearing what God is saying to you. It's that simple and, for that reason, the Church needs to help as many people as possible get out of their familiar comfort zones so they can obtain a new frame of reference and better perspective. Here are a few other reasons why the Church should actively and strategically send people out or provide meaningful work and/or ministry opportunities.

1. **They come home more effective Christians**. People returning from mission trips usually have a better handle on ministry priorities, are more confident, and serve in the local church more effectively. They are equipped to go back out again, armed with the experience of what people really need instead of what they *think* they may need.

2. **Churches need to obey the Great Commission.** The Great Commission applies no matter how limited or poor a church and its members may be. Jesus was clear that all believers must go. Since there are two billion people on the planet who have never heard the gospel once, everyone must do something to reach the lost, not only across the street but also around the world.

3. **Short-term missions can lead to people being called to long-term missions**. When people go, they often discover they are assigned to fulfill their purpose in other lands. Mission opportunities, both at home and abroad, give people a chance to be involved in work and ministry to see what they can do. When they see what they are and do is more valuable there than back home, they can correctly conclude God is showing them where they need to invest their lives and purpose.

4. **When people travel in teams to a foreign place,**

the real person comes out—for good or bad. This gives coaches and mentors plenty of chances to address problems that could possibly hinder people in fulfilling their purpose down the road. We need to find ways for people to play under game conditions, so to speak, so we can better direct their purpose development.

5. **Short-term missions will lead to more training opportunities before and after the people go and come back.** There can be language classes, cross-cultural ministry classes, and meetings where those who want to go on the next trip can hear firsthand reports of what they need to do to prepare as well as what they will do when they arrive at their destination.

I have mentioned that there should be many opportunities for training in the local church beyond just theological or biblical training. May I suggest one more seminar that would be appropriate for almost anyone, and that is a seminar on how to start a nonprofit corporation and raise money for that organization. When a church teaches and promotes purpose, there is no way that church, movement, or denomination can fund all the purpose expressions that will emanate from their midst.

Consequently, the church needs to equip and train people to raise their own support and start their own organizations to carry on the work. Most people believe having their own nonprofit is impossible or beyond their reach, but it's not. They can use their organization to obtain grants and corporate contributions, and to solicit financial help from individuals and churches for trips, relief work, construction, feeding programs, etc.

And while we are on the subject of business, the church also needs to provide advice for people who want to start their own businesses. Some of the businesses will help people fund their mission work. Other businesses will be the actual mission, for the enterprise someone starts may be the practical expression of that person's purpose. When businesses are successful, people prosper, and the church will prosper, too.

b) . . . and to carry out any other activity their purpose dictates and faith allows.

What I have described here are elements we know. When people engage their purpose, they come up with ideas for what has never been done before. We therefore lack the words or concepts to even talk about what some people of purpose will ultimately succeed in doing. Therefore, churches must provide legal assistance for people to patent and trademark ideas. People may need the kind of training and encouragement that isn't available from any church member or friend, so the church may need to scout around for the necessary counsel and help.

The church can provide coaches and mentors for those pursuing missions and business, but these mentors must know what they are doing. They must be spiritual people with some track record of success. I say that because when I was one of many pastors in a church in a southern city, members were encouraged to submit and discuss their ideas with their pastors. The problem was that many of the pastors were inexperienced or spoke into life situations for which they had no expertise and therefore had no business addressing. We have to be careful when we place the mantle of mentor or coach upon someone to ensure they can really help people.

And finally, this step requires that people be trained in the fine art of trusting the Lord. If God assigns purpose, He can provide for purpose, too. People must be taught to dream and not let the seeming impossibilities of their dreams stop them. That means they must hear about others and from others in the present or the past, people who did or are doing great feats for God, with God, and through God. They need to have their faith stretched but not overwhelmed by hearing stories of people with whom they can identify, who can encourage their faith.

Purpose is hard work. There is no such thing as a spiritual lottery where God is concerned. There is no one financial offering that can bring you what only a lifetime of diligent work can bring. Churches need to help people understand this truth. Then the people need to prepare and train practically and spiritually for challenges and ultimate success; and they need to be encouraged to do this from the pulpit and in one-on-one sessions. This may even mean some members become less available for the regular tasks of the church so they can have time freed up to learn, grow, and prepare for their future purpose.

Let me give you another example of the kind of work I believe churches should do to help people find their purpose. I was once on staff at a church where a family that was a long-standing member was frustrated with their role in the church and in life itself. They were about to leave the church when I met with them, identified what they were looking for, and asked them for time to come up with a plan before they made their final decision to move on. Let's call the couple Sam and Rachel.

I met with church leadership and we came up with a plan to offer Sam and Rachel the position of missionary interns at an annual pay that was below poverty level. This represented a 90% reduction in salary, but they accepted the position! We then set out a one-year plan to help them find their purpose. That plan included them traveling to four specific countries to explore the possibilities of relocating there. They also attended all our staff meetings. They visited the first three countries but came back saying, "That's not it." Then the visited the fourth, came home convinced it was God's will, and just recently returned from serving in that country almost 25 years.

Of course, this holds all kinds of implications for the local church. It requires someone who understands how to help people carry out God's purpose. It means that the church is close enough to their members to know what God is saying to them and will then take it to heart and follow through to help people overcome obstacles to do innovative things for God's kingdom. I don't believe purpose preparation will impoverish the church in any way. Jesus knows how to build His church, universal and local, and needs leaders who can cooperate and not hinder His plan for the Church or the people in it.

CHAPTER 5
QUESTIONS FOR DISCUSSION OR STUDY

1. Read Proverbs 14:23. How does this verse apply to the concept of the spiritual lottery and shortcuts to success?

2. Have you ever considered starting your own organization or company? What would it be?

3. Do you think the Church should equip its members to function on their own, or should the Church only look to build up its own work and ministries?

4. Is lack of money really the major problem churches and/or individuals face in their quest to be effective? What are the other obstacles that may be standing between them and success in the will of God?

5. Does or should the Church have any role in equipping people to start businesses or ministries? How do you understand Psalm 24:1? Is it the job of the church to extend God's rule to every area of life and work?

6. What does Hebrews 11:6 say? Is faith an event or a lifestyle? What role should the Church play to encourage people to have and exercise faith?

7. Take out a sheet of paper. Make a list of all the training you would like to have if you had the time that would make a difference in what you could do for the Lord.

8. One the other side of the paper, list all the training sessions

your church could offer that may be of interest to its members and the community.

CHAOS OUT OF ORDER

REFORMATION STEP THREE:
HELP LEADERS BE PRODUCTIVE IN THEIR PURPOSE AS THEY OVERSEE HOLY SPIRIT CHAOS CREATED BY PEOPLE PURSUING AND FULFILLING THEIR PURPOSE.

Now that we have covered the first two steps, it's time to turn our attention once again to the issue of church leadership. When I refer to church leaders, this includes pastors, paid staff, elders, bishops, vicars, deacons, department heads, volunteers, or anyone who is leading someone to accomplish something in a church setting. If you are in doubt as to whether or not you are a leader for the purpose of this discussion, assume that you are or will be. Eventually when these Eight Steps take effect, we will need all the leaders we can possibly find!

To begin, let's look at two passages for examples of what I mean by Holy Spirit chaos. First, let's read Acts 6:1-7.

In those days when the number of disciples was increasing, the Grecian Jews among them complained against the Hebraic Jews because their widows were being overlooked in the daily distribution of food. So the Twelve gathered all the disciples together and said, "It would not be right for us to neglect the ministry of the word of God in order to wait on tables. Brothers, choose seven men from among you who are known to be full of the Spirit and wisdom. We will turn this responsibility over to them and will give our attention to prayer and the ministry of the word." This proposal pleased the whole group. They chose Stephen, a man full of faith and of the Holy Spirit; also Philip, Procorus, Nicanor, Timon, Parmenas, and Nicolas from Antioch, a convert to Judaism. They presented these men to the apostles, who prayed and laid their hands on them. So the word of God spread. The number of disciples in Jerusalem increased rapidly, and a large number of priests became obedient to the faith.

The following points regarding the verses above are pertinent to Holy Spirit chaos:

1. Each apostle knew his own purpose, which prevented him from being sucked into the crisis of the day. In this instance, the crisis was the growing number of non-Hebraic widows who were being overlooked in the benevolent distributions.

2. The leaders had their own work to do that no one else could do as they could.

3. The growth of the church caused problems. This was not an indication that something was wrong with the church, but that they were doing something right.

4. While the leaders listened to the voice of the people, they put the problem right back on the people. When the people basically said, "Someone needs to do something," the leaders made them the "someone" who needed to be involved.

5. The leaders determined the people should hold an election. They trusted the work of the Spirit in the people to such an extent that they had complete confidence they would make the correct decision.

6. The church had an existing pool of talent, if I can use that phrase, from which they could draw additional leadership. These men were full of the Spirit and wisdom.

7. The leaders knew how to delegate and did not have to do everything.

There is much more I could say about this passage, which has become the cornerstone for each purpose message I deliver. The one additional point I would like to emphasize is found in verse seven, which says the word of God continued to spread and the church grew. This was because those men knew how to stay focused and flow with the unexpected, what I call the chaos, that tends to arise in the life of every church.

VISION AND DOCTRINE

The early church leaders did not have a vision for what kind of church they wanted to have. Instead, they flowed with the vision Jesus had for the church. This meant they had to be flexible with what took place but rigid where doctrine was concerned. Today we sometimes take the opposite approach: we are rigid with our vision and flexible with our doctrine!

This is important because rigidity where vision is concerned will cause leaders to dismiss those in their midst who cannot contribute toward the accomplishment of that vision.

When someone has a desire to help the church, leaders often try to fit that person into a few predetermined jobs. I have often said you can do anything you want in a church, as long as it is ushering, choir, or nursery. If you can't help there, then many churches don't know what to do with you (unless perhaps you are a missionary).

I once worked with a church that had a member come forward with a plan to develop a ministry toward students from foreign lands who were in their city. The church deliberated long and hard because this "burden" was not in the scope of the leaders' vision for the church. What's more, the member had asked for some money to fund the project! That usually causes any leadership team to say no automatically. To this church's credit, however, the leaders said yes, and before long, many of those foreign students came to know the Lord.

This story epitomizes what I refer to as Holy Spirit chaos, for the ministry idea bubbled up from the bottom, from among the membership. It did not come from the top. When you make room for the Holy Spirit working in the people, the Spirit does not have to follow any predetermined rules, protocol, strategic plan, or vision. Leaders who want to control the process can do that easily, but they are then restricted to what they alone can see instead of accessing all that could be. The second promised passage that exemplifies Step Three is found in Acts 13:1-3.

> In the church at Antioch there were prophets and teachers: Barnabas, Simeon called Niger, Lucius of Cyrene, Manaen (who had been brought up with Herod the tetrarch) and Saul. While they were worshiping the Lord and fasting, the Holy Spirit said, "Set apart for me Barnabas and Saul for the work to which I have called them." So after they had fasted and prayed, they placed their hands on them and sent them off.

Barnabas played a key role in the revival that was taking place at Antioch and had brought Saul in as his assistant. At some point, the leaders took time to minister to the Lord in prayer and fasting, and the Holy Spirit spoke that it was time to send Barnabas and Saul out as missionaries. The Spirit did not ask permission; He did not seem to care what Barnabas and Saul were doing in the church at that point or what their absence would mean to the team left behind. The Spirit spoke and the people were expected to respond. I am not sure this mission was part of the church's vision, but that didn't matter once the Spirit had spoken.

In the first example from Acts 6, we saw how a problem created a need for an entirely new level of leadership. In this second example, we see how the Spirit moved people around according to His own plan and purpose. You can understand how chaotic this kind of ministry can seem to those who want to plan their work and work their plan. Yet purpose creates this kind of disorder for which God does not apologize.

Please note that this kind of disorder is not the same as confusion. Clarity of direction was displayed in both instances, but the direction was a shift from the way the church had been conducting business. From a human perspective it could appear to be chaotic, but from God's perspective, it made perfect sense. This is why Step Three requires that leaders learn to live with and respond to Holy Spirit chaos.

CHANGE: HOLY SPIRIT CHAOS

Responding to this kind of chaos requires constant change and adjustment. As I said in chapter three, the church should eat change for breakfast, for we are the Spirit-led people. Yet I have found the church is not particularly adept at managing change, and it starts at the top.

Years ago, I heard Peter Drucker, father of modern management studies, say, "The only way to manage change is to initiate it." We should not have change imposed on us but rather have the courage and faith to seek and initiate it. Once we see change as the norm and not the exception, we can help manage it by taking the following steps:

1. Have a plan of succession for leaders, even if they are the founders. That person will not live forever and may be called to another work at any time, whether they like it or seek it. This process, however, does not involve the divine right of kings. If a family member is God's choice to succeed, that's fine. If not, then no one has the right to impose his or her personal will or choice in the succession plan, even the founder of the work.

2. Everyone should be training and preparing their successor no matter *what* task they are doing in the church.

3. Have some means by which leadership can hear and process what the Spirit is saying to the people. After all, if the leaders are doing their jobs, the people will hear from God. Isn't it important to know what He is saying even if He chooses not to first speak it to the leaders?

4. Leaders should always be evaluating what they are doing well and not so well. This will enable them to seek better answers and more anointed and talented people to lead the church ministries. Every church needs to have feedback mechanisms that will help them understand their own effectiveness.

5. There should be an ongoing training program that improves the leadership skills of members and leaders, which we will discuss more in

chapter eleven. This will enable them to face, embrace, and prosper in the kind of shifting environment and seeming chaos the Spirit creates.

I am not against planning. I have found, however, that our plans are not infallible, and they are certainly based on incomplete and imperfect knowledge. My own experience has shown that those plans need to be revisited and revised about every six months, since one new move of the Spirit can create a whole new world of activity. A person in their purpose can create the same dynamic, just like when Barnabas and Saul were set apart for their own purpose.

Concerning our responses to change, vision, chaos, and the people, the proper attitude is essential. When leaders believe they own the work and the people, they will tend to be resistant to change and can harden their hearts to it, seeing suggested change as disloyalty or rebellion. With that in mind, Step Four will address this "owner's attitude" that exists among some leaders today.

CHAPTER 6
QUESTIONS FOR DISCUSSION OR STUDY

1. Read Acts 6:1-7. What lessons for leadership can you find in that passage?

2. What lessons are there in Acts 6:1-7 for you? Are you waiting on tables, doing good work that isn't the best you can do? What are you prepared to do about that?

3. How do you respond to change?

4. How well does your church process change?

5. Is your church growing? Why or why not?

6. Are you growing? Why or why not?

7. How can you or your church obtain more feedback on your/their performance? Do you even want feedback? Does your church?

8. What is your personal leadership development plan? Does it include reading, classes, travel, new growth experiences, and rest?

9. Does your church have a personal development plan for each staff member and volunteer? How about a succession plan for leadership? Do you have one for the position you have? Remember, no one lives forever. You also want to be ready for the new opportunities that will come when God opens the door.

10. How does your church keep track of what God is saying to the people? How do you track what He is saying to you?

ALL OF US
ARE SMARTER
THAN ONE OF US

REFORMATION STEP FOUR:
HELP LEADERS AND GOVERNING BODIES
MOVE FROM ATTITUDES OF OWNERSHIP TO
ATTITUDES OF SERVANT LEADERSHIP AND
STEWARDSHIP.

The memory of a meeting I once attended will stay with me for the rest of my life. I was with a group of elders who had oversight for a church in decline. The membership and finances were half of what they were a few years earlier. I had been invited to see if I could help create a strategy for improvement—order out of chaos, which is my purpose.

During the gathering, it became clear the elder board

was divided, and many of them were arrogant. I remember one man sticking out his chest when he declared, "I'm an elder. Why wasn't I informed about this particular issue?"

At that point, I responded, "If I were an elder in this group, I would not be bragging. I would have resigned long ago!" I then asked an experienced businessman sitting at the table, "If this were a business, what would you do?" He immediately responded, "I would shake up the board while there was still something to shake." Unfortunately, our meeting was unproductive, no decisions were made, and the church limped along, suffering loss after agonizing loss until another church bought their building and incorporated what little was left of the former church into the buying church's membership.

This is only one example of what I have observed in many churches in various countries. Sometimes the fault lies with the elders or the senior pastor; at other times it is the founding pastor, the pastor's wife, or even the music minister. At some point, someone begins to talk about "*my* church" or "*my* staff." That is a sure sign the leader does not see himself (or herself) as a servant but rather as an owner. We all know that owners act much differently than servants.

I described in chapter two the role that Robert Greenleaf played in my own leadership transformation and reformation. Before Greenleaf, I was grappling with my tendencies toward heavy-handedness and control, without making much progress on the cause or the cure. Greenleaf gave me the necessary tools and insight to move forward.

I have used feedback profiles from a company called The Leadership Circle. This particular instrument gives an assessment in twenty-nine key areas of a leader's style. The person being assessed chooses people to fill out an anonymous online survey, after which the scores are compiled. Warning! These profiles are revealing and should not be employed unless one is serious about obtaining accurate feedback for growth and development.

My 360-degree leadership profile let me know that my efforts, by God's grace, have not been in vain. I scored very low on control and much higher on relationships than I ever thought possible thirty years ago. Let me repeat: I am not against leadership. Every leader plays an important role in God's plan. I don't believe, however, that any leader has everything needed for any organization. I subscribe to the maxim that states:

- All of us are smarter and more spiritual than one of us, but. . .
- All of us are *not* as smart or spiritual as we need to be.

Did you ever notice how spiritual the people were and how unspiritual the leaders were in Jesus' day? Let me give you a few examples to prove the truth of that statement:

1. The people knew that John was a prophet; the leaders did not.

"John's baptism—where did it come from? Was it from heaven, or from men?" They discussed it among themselves and said, "If we say, 'From heaven,' he will ask, 'Then why didn't you believe him?' But if we say, 'From men'—we are afraid of the people, for they all hold that John was a prophet" (Matthew 21:25-26).

2. The people knew that Jesus was the Messiah; the leaders did not.

When the chief priests and the Pharisees heard Jesus' parables, they knew he was talking about them. They looked for a way to arrest him, but they were afraid of the crowd because the people held that he was a prophet (Matthew 21:45-46).

3. The people knew that the apostles had performed a great miracle; the leaders wanted to kill them for it.

> When they saw the courage of Peter and John and realized that they were unschooled, ordinary men, they were astonished and they took note that these men had been with Jesus. But since they could see the man who had been healed standing there with them, there was nothing they could say. So they ordered them to withdraw from the Sanhedrin and then conferred together. "What are we going to do with these men?" they asked. "Everybody living in Jerusalem knows they have done an outstanding miracle, and we cannot deny it. But to stop this thing from spreading any further among the people, we must warn these men to speak no longer to anyone in this name" (Acts 4:13-17).

Being a leader was no guarantee of being "correct." I am not suggesting the crowd is always correct, but neither am I dismissing them because they are always wrong. The leaders in Jesus' day were intelligent, well-educated men, but they needed to expand their team to include a variety of people with diverse perspectives. Only God is perfect, and we serve Him and ask for His wisdom. He can give it to whomever He wishes, whether they are non-leaders or bishops. That is up to Him, and our role is to seek it from whatever source He has chosen and respond accordingly.

There is collective wisdom and spirituality in a group of leaders, but the group constantly needs to expand to include more perspectives and gifts. When the few at the top limit their contact and input from others, the group and church will ultimately suffer. Therefore, elders, pastors, and deacons are essential but must not be impressed with their own position, otherwise they will lord it over those whom they are appointed to lead. It's that simple.

What can leaders do to combat this most human of tendencies? One thing they can do is immerse themselves in a study of Scripture that describes what servant leaders are and do. They can supplement their studies with some very good books on leadership that contain God's truths in a non-biblical format.

I have often heard spiritual leaders say, "You cannot run the church like IBM," and they are correct. Yet to eliminate all leadership wisdom simply because it does not come from a spiritual person is foolishness. For the last twenty years, non-church leaders have written most of the leadership books that have spoken to me and added the most to my understanding of leadership. It is my job to test what they write to ensure it can be "baptized" with scriptural principles. If those truths do not violate Scripture, then those truths are indeed God's truths and can be applied to any leadership role. For now, let's look at some important verses to help leaders understand Step Four:

> "Woe to the shepherds who are destroying and scattering the sheep of my pasture!" declares the Lord. Therefore this is what the Lord, the God of Israel, says to the shepherds who tend my people: "Because you have scattered my flock and driven them away and have not bestowed care on them, I will bestow punishment on you for the evil you have done," declares the Lord. "I myself will gather the remnant of my flock out of all the countries where I have driven them and will bring them back to their pasture, where they will be fruitful and increase in number. I will place shepherds over them who will tend them, and they will no longer be afraid or terrified, nor will any be missing," declares the Lord (Jeremiah 23:1-4).

This word came to Ezekiel about the shepherds of Israel:

The word of the Lord came to me: "Son of man, prophesy against the **shepherds** of Israel; prophesy and say to them: 'This is what the Sovereign Lord says: Woe to the **shepherds** of Israel who only take care of themselves! Should not **shepherds** take care of the flock? You eat the curds, clothe yourselves with the wool and slaughter the choice animals, but you do not take care of the flock. You have not strengthened the weak or healed the sick or bound up the injured. You have not brought back the strays or searched for the lost. You have ruled them harshly and brutally. So they were scattered because there was no **shepherd**, and when they were scattered they became food for all the wild animals. My sheep wandered over all the mountains and on every high hill. They were scattered over the whole earth, and no one searched or looked for them.

"'Therefore, you **shepherds**, hear the word of the Lord: As surely as I live, declares the Sovereign Lord, because my flock lacks a **shepherd** and so has been plundered and has become food for all the wild animals, and because my **shepherds** did not search for my flock but cared for themselves rather than for my flock, therefore, O **shepherds**, hear the word of the Lord: This is what the Sovereign Lord says: I am against the **shepherds** and will hold them accountable for my flock. I will remove them from tending the flock so that the **shepherds** can no longer feed themselves. I will rescue my flock from their mouths, and it will no longer be food for them.

"'For this is what the Sovereign Lord says: I myself will search for my sheep and look after them. As a **shepherd** looks after his scattered flock when he is with them, so will I look after my sheep. I will rescue them from all the places where they were scattered on a day of clouds and darkness. I will bring them out from the nations and gather them from the countries, and I will bring them into their own land. I will pasture them on the mountains of Israel, in the ravines and in all the settlements in the land. I will tend them in a good pasture, and the mountain heights of

Israel will be their grazing land. There they will lie down in good grazing land, and there they will feed in a rich pasture on the mountains of Israel. I myself will tend my sheep and have them lie down, declares the Sovereign Lord. I will search for the lost and bring back the strays. I will bind up the injured and strengthen the weak, but the sleek and the strong I will destroy. I will shepherd the flock with justice" (Ezekiel 34:1-16 emphasis added).

There is enough in those two passages to require two reformations. I am always challenged and humbled when I read these verses, for I am reminded that leaders are accountable to the Chief Shepherd for the job they do—and He is watching closely. I own no sheep, no church, no position, no favor, and no place of prominence. I am called to serve, and I do so not because I am superior spiritually but because God in His grace has called me to care for His people.

Shepherds are to feed the sheep in pastures where they will grow. Too often, we have taught people how to help a church grow and have neglected educating them how they can grow personally. In other words, we should not use the sheep to build our kingdom but to help build God's kingdom. The Lord extends His kingdom as people express their purpose both in and out of the church. I am not against church growth, but church growth takes place as depicted in Acts 6 when people come to know God's purpose for their lives.

The most important practice to enhance the reformation of leadership and consequently advance Step Four is that leaders need to listen. That's all—just listen. When I go to churches, I spend time with the people, and they disclose their dreams to me. We talk about their purpose and they share their stories and experiences. I then go to the leadership with my report of what I heard and what it may require going forward.

People talk to me because often no one else is listening, and they are hungry to talk. I realize one person cannot do all the listening, especially as the church grows. That is why we need to expand leadership and equip leaders to be in touch with the Lord through the people. Those leaders need to hear what the Spirit is saying and then make recommendations of how leadership can move according to what they hear.

How can men and women in charge improve their listening? First and foremost, you need to stop talking long enough to listen. If you talk more than twenty-five percent of any meeting, then you aren't listening! The next step is to learn to ask better questions, open-ended questions that draw people out and make them think. Then summarize what you have learned from any meeting and determine a way forward to help that person. If you can't carry out these action steps and you are a leader, then find someone who is gifted to do so and rely on them to give you feedback—while you develop the skill to do so yourself.

If you are content, however, to preach and control, to speak and not listen, to own and not serve, then every step I outlined is futile. The reformation I foresee isn't based on leadership; it's based on the Spirit's work in the people. If you can't handle that, then you won't ever see it. And if you don't see it, then you can't go to Step Five, which once again puts the burden on leadership to establish a standard of excellence that makes people eager to serve and participate.

CHAPTER 7
QUESTIONS FOR DISCUSSION OR STUDY

1. Lord Action once said, "There is no worse heresy than that the office sanctifies the holder of it." What did he mean by this? How does it relate to the fact that the people often knew more than their leaders in Jesus' day?

2. Read 1 Corinthians 12:13-31. How does this relate to the concept of leaders and followers in the church? Do you think leaders may actually need to follow more than they lead?

3. Read Colossians 3:16. Does this pertain to leaders or to everyone?

4. Read Hebrews 13:17. Is everyone equal in the sight of God in the church? What legitimate authority does a church leader have?

5. Read James 1:19. Notice that we often tend to be quick to do the wrong thing and slow to the correct behavior. How would you evaluate yourself as a listener?

6. How well does your church listen to one another, especially those who are not in leadership positions? How can you improve? Do you want to improve?

7. Read Ezekiel 34:1-16 one more time. What are the major roles that shepherds should have according to this passage? How well do you fulfill those roles? How well does your church leadership do in those areas? What can you do to improve?

8. What are you doing to expand the ministry or work team on which you serve? Are you hearing from all groups— young, old, minorities, women, and others who don't think or look like you?

WHEN GOOD ISN'T
GOOD ENOUGH

REFORMATION STEP FIVE:
DEVELOP SERVICES, SUNDAY SCHOOLS, KID'S
CHURCH, YOUTH MEETINGS, AND EVEN
COMMITTEE MEETINGS THAT PEOPLE WANT TO
ATTEND BECAUSE THEY INVOLVE A SPIRIT OF
EXCELLENCE AND THE UNEXPECTED.

When I first started teaching what I call the five Gold Mine Principles outlined in my book, *Life Is a Gold Mine: Can You Dig It?*, I entitled my section on goal setting, "Be Careful Where You Dig: When Good Isn't Good Enough." One time that session was mistakenly advertised as, "When God Isn't Good Enough," and people came to see what I had to say about that! Of course, God is always good enough, but often our efforts to serve Him and express His goodness fall woefully short.

Excellence is not about having the finest equipment or wearing the most expensive clothes when doing something for God. Nothing is necessarily wrong with those two practices, but they actually fall far short of my concept of excellence. I discuss my concept more fully in the Appendix, but it will suffice for now that I define excellence as "doing all you do from a right heart and in a manner worthy of God!"

That definition shows we have a long way to go in the pursuit of church excellence. Remember, I am not talking about perfection but instead an attitude that is always seeking to improve with the best interests of others in mind. One way we can pursue this kind of excellence is to develop systems of meaningful feedback to help us measure what we do and how effective it is in reaching other people.

I know this opens a can of worms, since many people shun any kind of evaluation of spiritual things, saying that the results are in God's hands—if He was and is pleased, the job was well done, even if no one thought much of it. Others say if only one person was helped, then the effort was worth it. While this sounds spiritual, is it really? Remember when we looked at Acts 6, the passage ended with verse seven:

> So the word of God spread. The number of disciples
> in Jerusalem increased rapidly, and a large number
> of priests became obedient to the faith (Acts 6:7).

The results of the leaders staying focused and deacons being elected were that the Word of God spread and many came to know Him. Numbers are one, and only one, feedback mechanism that can help a church determine how well it is doing. What the numbers indicate can only be determined by the church's leadership, but the numbers always reveal something. Let's consider another important passage, the misinterpretation of which has hindered individuals and churches from pursuing greatness and excellence in their service to God:

I am the true vine, and my Father is the gardener. He cuts off every branch in me that bears no fruit, while every branch that does bear fruit he prunes so that it will be even more fruitful. You are already clean because of the word I have spoken to you. Remain in me, and I will remain in you. No branch can bear fruit by itself; it must remain in the vine. Neither can you bear fruit unless you remain in me.

I am the vine; you are the branches. If a man remains in me and I in him, he will bear much fruit; apart from me you can do nothing. If anyone does not remain in me, he is like a branch that is thrown away and withers; such branches are picked up, thrown into the fire and burned. If you remain in me and my words remain in you, ask whatever you wish, and it will be given you. This is to my Father's glory, that you bear much fruit, showing yourselves to be my disciples (John 15:1-8).

I have been warned many times by pastors and saints not to do anything outside of Christ and the will of God. I have worked with some people who were so afraid they would miss the Lord and do something out of God's purpose that they often ended up missing the Lord, in my estimation, by doing nothing! They were so afraid of doing the *wrong* thing they did *no* thing. Some saints believe that when they become more patient, don't cuss, and don't watch "bad" movies, they are being fruitful in the center of God's will. Is that the message of John 15?

If apart from Christ we can do nothing, as individuals or churches, then in Him *we should do something—maybe a lot of things!* If apart from the vine, we can bear no fruit, then should we not bear much fruit as part of the vine? We have made the entire emphasis of John 15 negative when it should be challenging and positive. If we abide in the vine, our prayers should and will be answered. If we abide in the vine, every believer will bear fruit, not just *some* fruit but *much* fruit. Much fruit honors God, and that implies little fruit dishonors Him. And much fruit will lead to more fruit, since God will prune so that even more fruit is possible.

If leaders and followers were clear on this issue, they could and would hold one another to a new standard of excellence and fruitfulness. The standard would not only ask, "Did you steal?" but also, for example, "How many orphans are you supporting from the wages you earn?" If we agreed that God wanted fruit and wanted it in abundance, we would no longer be content with a pleasant, peaceful Sunday service where the meeting went off without a hitch. We would communicate a much different gospel with different standards for worship and behavior for the people of God. An expanded understanding of John 15 will free leaders to focus on productivity and excellence of results without embarrassment or ambivalence.

WILL THE REAL FRUIT PLEASE STAND UP?

A biblical leader can help dispel the myth that fruit is only what happens on the inside of a believer or church. While the fruit of holiness is beautiful and necessary, it is not the only fruit God requires. An effective leader will not settle for anything less than the maximum growth the Holy Spirit desires for His part of the body and the members in it. The leader need only refer to Ephesians 2:10 to encourage believers that their fruit is to be tangible, visible, and therefore measurable: "For we are God's workmanship, created in Christ Jesus to do good works, which God prepared in advance for us to do."

The fruit should not be limited to any one category because John 15 does not put any restrictions or limitations on the fruit. Churches and individuals should be producing growth and increase in areas of personal holiness while also advancing their God-given purpose so others can come to know

77

Jesus. Practical needs also should be met through orphanages, published books, new businesses, and creative ministries that impact the world. Leaders can bolster the strength of their case for fruit by also referring to something else Jesus said:

> "I tell you the truth, anyone who has faith in me will do what I have been doing. He will do even greater things than these, because I am going to the Father. And I will do whatever you ask in my name, so that the Son may bring glory to the Father. You may ask me for anything in my name, and I will do it" (John 14:12-14).

Whatever one interprets to be Jesus' greatest works, we should all be performing even greater ones. Jesus never opened a business or hospital, wrote or published a book, built or planted a local church, or established orphanages and benevolent funds to feed the hungry. He didn't do any of those things because He left them for His followers to do, both in unison as a body and as individuals. It's not that Jesus could not do those things, but He restricted His activity to do them through and with His people.

Leaders who do not apologize for or theologize away God's expectation of fruit but hold that as the expected standard will be well on their way to bearing fruit as leaders and helping followers do the same. It is God's will for His people to bear all kinds of fruit and enjoy the synergies of a church walking under the lordship of Christ in the power of their individual and corporate purpose.

Again, numbers are not the only or the most important measure of excellence. Each church should and must define success in terms of their mission and purpose. What measurements have you set for your personal work or that of your church? If not numbers, then what? How will you know if and when you are hitting the mark?

Notice that Step Five requires that all gatherings to

have a sense of excellence, expectation, and the unexpected. By the unexpected, I don't mean that people must manifest bizarre behavior under what they say is the Spirit's leading. It doesn't mean public meetings must last four hours. It means the results of what we do should always exceed expectations—and expectations should be high. If you must force your youth to attend their youth meetings, for example, then you have a problem in the youth department, and it must be addressed and remedied. The same holds true for every activity and event across the church.

There is only one way to get anointed results in or out of the church and that is to find what people are anointed to do and help them do it. People must be put in the place where they have the best chance for success. Too often we have placed people where there was the greatest need, whether or not they had the gifts to function in that position, and then wondered why we were not getting supernatural returns.

We put people in the nursery who didn't like children, assigned unfriendly people as ushers, and staffed the youth department with volunteers who had no gifting to work with youth. We also provided them with little or no training. It is no wonder then that we get "unanointed" or less than excellent results. God's presence is released when people bring His presence with them to what they do and that presence is usually identified by joy doing the work.

So what do we do when we need someone to work in the nursery, for example? I suggest we ask someone to serve for six months and monitor his or her performance. We allow them to be honest and admit if they are not happy. We give them some training, but we don't try to force or manipulate them into doing a job for God or the church. At the end of the six months, we thank them for their services and allow them to move on if that is what they want to do.

If people are unhappy in their assigned role, I advise

them not to deny how they are feeling. They can acknowledge they are doing this job for a season, even though it is not their comfort or sweet spot. They thank God for the opportunity to serve and do His will, but I do not allow them to talk themselves out of how they feel. At the same time, I try to help them find a more suitable position that will better utilize their gifts and purpose.

Churches have attempted to rectify the problem Step Five addresses by attending conferences, where those who have experienced success share their wisdom with those who have not enjoyed success or who want more of it. This has led to a different kind of problem where people and leaders look for easy answers by mimicking someone else's program or solutions. I will outline the remedy for that tendency in the next chapter.

CHAPTER 8
QUESTIONS FOR DISCUSSION OR STUDY

1. Read John 15:1-8. Where have you put the emphasis, on being in the vine or being careful not to be apart from the vine?

2. What is your view on your prayers being answered in this context?

3. Do you agree with the point that fruit is more than holiness? Do you think what Christians do can and should be measured?

4. How do you measure success and fruitfulness? How does your church measure them? Should they even be measured?

5. How do you feel about doing greater works than Jesus did as mentioned in John 14:12-14? Do you agree it is more than doing the miracles Jesus did, like raising the dead or healing crippled people? Does doing "greater works" apply to you? Your church?

6. How committed are you to excellence as defined in this chapter? Do you agree with the definition? Can you think of a better one you are willing to follow?

7. Are you doing what you do best? Are the people in your church? How can you all do better?

8. Do you tolerate boring meetings, whether you are leading or participating? What can you do to improve? Do you force your family or followers to endure boring meetings? Why is that?

WHEN NOT TO FOLLOW THE LEADER

REFORMATION STEP SIX:
MOVE FROM FADS, COPYCAT PROGRAMS, AND TRITE AND PHONY RITUALS, TRADITIONS, AND DOCTRINES TO INNOVATIVE INITIATIVES IN THE SPIRIT OF (BUT EXCEEDING THE RESULTS OF) THE EARLY CHURCH.

When I was a child, my friends and I played follow-the-leader from time to time. We had fun as we mimicked whatever the person leading felt inclined to do. Unfortunately, many churches have opted to take this route and play that game, and it has not worked out very well. What worked for a particular leader or church movement can't always be transferred to another leader or group. They may try to take someone else's hard work and gifting and apply it in their own church situation, but eventually the enthusiasm fades—and then it's time for another conference. The practice of wanting to find shortcuts to success or to overcome problems they are facing seldom works by copying someone else.

I know I've stated it before, but we should be known as the "change people," for we are Spirit-led. The Spirit doesn't lead us to change for change sake, but He leads us in new ways to take advantage of new opportunities to reach and touch more people. In addition to being change agents, we should also be the most creative people in the world.

We have the Spirit of wisdom in our midst, so we should not have to copy anyone to do what we do in the church. That doesn't mean we won't learn from others or even emulate what they do from time to time. It does mean that when we emulate them, however, we need to make sure we have adapted the change to our particular church or culture so it is a good fit for where we want to apply it. Let's look again at the passage from Acts 6:1-7 that we looked at in chapter six.

> In those days when the number of disciples was in-creasing, the Grecian Jews among them complained against the Hebraic Jews because their widows were being overlooked in the daily distribution of food. So the Twelve gathered all the disciples together and said, "It would not be right for us to neglect the ministry of the word of God in order to wait on tables. Brothers, choose seven men from among you who are known to be full of the Spirit and wisdom. We will turn this responsibility over to them and will give our attention to prayer and the ministry of the word."
>
> This proposal pleased the whole group. They chose Stephen, a man full of faith and of the Holy Spirit; also Philip, Procorus, Nicanor, Timon, Parmenas, and Nicolas from Antioch, a convert to Judaism.

They presented these men to the apostles, who prayed and laid their hands on them. So the word of God spread. The number of disciples in Jerusalem increased rapidly, and a large number of priests became obedient to the faith.

Most churches that have deacons use this passage to justify the fact that they do and there is nothing wrong with that. Yet I think there is more to this passage than just instituting deacons. The early church encountered a problem that had never been faced, and they came up with a creative solution that has lasted for centuries.

Now there are some who look at that passage and study it as a relic of how God worked in the early church. I see it as the gateway to and model for the future. Just like those in Acts 6, the leaders and people today should pioneer creative, innovative solutions to problems that the church and the world are encountering. After all, we have the creative Spirit in our midst, powerful spiritual gifts, and the promise that nothing is impossible with God. Look at this passage from Proverbs and tell me it doesn't speak to the creative energy available to us in the Lord:

The Lord brought me forth as the first of his works, before his deeds of old; I was appointed from eternity, from the beginning, before the world began. When there were no oceans, I was given birth, when there were no springs abounding with water; before the mountains were settled in place, before the hills, I was given birth, before he made the earth or its fields or any of the dust of the world. I was there when he set the heavens in place, when he marked out the horizon on the face of the deep, when he established the clouds above and fixed securely the fountains of the deep, when he gave the sea its boundary so the waters would not overstep his command, and when he marked out the foundations of the earth.

Then I was the craftsman at his side. I was filled with delight day after day, rejoicing always in his presence, rejoicing in his whole world and delighting in mankind. Now then, my sons, listen to me; blessed are those who keep my ways. Listen to my instruction and be wise; do not ignore it. Blessed is the man who listens to me, watching daily at my doors, waiting at my doorway. For whoever finds me finds life and receives favor from the Lord. But whoever fails to find me harms himself; all who hate me love death (Proverbs 8:22-36).

Are there any other examples of creativity from which we can draw as we seek our new reformation? Of course, there are. Consider these examples:

- David fought Goliath while the army of God went through maneuvers but stayed out of harm's way. He did not fight Goliath with conventional means. He fought using what had worked with in the past, adapted for his present enemy.

- Jesus healed in a variety of ways—sometimes with spit, sometimes with a touch, other times with a word.

- Paul had to engage a Gentile world creatively with the message of the Jewish covenant fulfilled in Christ.

What's more, we have countless examples of believers down through the ages who sought, found, and applied creative solutions. The source of their ingenuity was their faith. Consider Florence Nightingale, Dr. Martin Luther King Jr., George Washington Carver, William Wilberforce, and David Livingstone, just to name just a few. Why can't the church once again produce creative ideas and innovative problem-solvers who know how to tap into the Spirit of wisdom?

The question at hand is this: In Acts 6 when the church chose deacons, did that act represent the exact model to follow, or was it expressing a concept we are to apply to the challenges we face today? I believe the latter is the case. Acts 6 models a concept and not just a rule. This is about more than every church having deacons; it is about everybody facing their challenges with faith and creativity, while staying true to the foundations of the faith.

Notice too the leaders found ways to involve the people in the process. The people voted on those who spearheaded the revised ministry to widows, and the people elected those who were Greek-speaking believers. The apostles then turned responsibility for the widows over to the duly-elected deacons. If you don't have people in your church who can do that, then you haven't done a good job of developing people. And if you are a member and aren't willing to be part of the solution to a problem or opportunity the church is facing, then you should not complain—and ask yourself why they don't want to be involved.

My church has a counseling department with two paid employees and numerous other counselors who are in private practice and are compensated for counseling appointments at the church as they are booked and paid for. The church has creative after-school programs to address educational needs. There is a café that serves hot lunches and food so people can meet and mingle (that's a nice word for fellowship). The cafeteria is open on Sunday and feeds hundreds of people. We currently have four services, with a chance for small group meetings after each service. The small groups have been creatively adapted to the church culture even though modeled after another successful church small-group program.

When I was on staff, I wanted to supplement the

church's creativity with my own. Here are some of the things I did.

1. Held quarterly purpose seminars that were free and open to the public. They were four hours in length and covered purpose, personality profiles, spiritual gifts, strengths and weaknesses, and creativity.

2. To help me facilitate those seminars, I recruited people to what I called the Divine Design Team. We met regularly to talk about purpose and how we could promote it in the congregation. Then they attended the seminars and sat at a table to facilitate questions and discussions. Each member was then available to meet with others one on one to help them apply what they had learned from the seminar.

3. I began a monthly creativity support meeting called G1: Living the Life of a Creator (G1 was short for Genesis 1, where God's creative nature is on display). People would assemble to share their creative work, get feedback, be encouraged, or give encouragement to others. We would also teach, pray, and discuss the concept of creativity. We have moved this session online since the pandemic began.

4. I launched a weekly blog radio show on which I would highlight people of purpose in the church to stimulate the vision and creativity of the listeners.

5. I began leading a group of people every year to Kenya to visit with my ministry partners there. Over time, a few people felt it was their purpose to accompany me every year. Some of them I

helped start their own nonprofit organizations so they could raise money and focus on a specific need they saw while there like widows, orphans, or community development

6. I founded public libraries in Kenya and collected books in the States to ship there. A team of people helped me collect, sort, package, and then ship the books to our Kenyan libraries.

7. When I left my church staff position, it was to start Urban Press to help people publish their stories and testimonies. I have been available to help anyone in the church publish, often at a reduced fee.

Now you may think, "Those ideas aren't particularly creative. Some churches already do them." If that is your thought, you are correct. Yet each of those ideas is not just a copycat program from another church. They were all creatively molded and applied to the particular mission of our church, my purpose, and the gifts and purpose of others. Those new initiatives didn't happen just because they were taking place in other churches. They happened because they were right for our church and for me. They didn't take place because I ordered them to exist, but because a consensus was reached that these programs were in the will of God and right for the people.

Each program did not mimic what others were saying or doing. They expressed the individuality of our church and the gifting represented by the membership. For example, not many people teach purpose the way I do. That isn't a boast, and I am not saying my way is the best way—but it is unique to me. I want to put my stamp on any church or program I am in. I want to make room for the voices of others while I make a place for my own.

Before we move on, I have one final point on this topic.

In this step I include the phrase, *"in the Spirit of (but exceeding the results of) the early church."* The early church had great success because God *wanted* them to succeed. His Spirit was in their midst and they proclaimed and modeled a new message with profound joy and zeal. Is that something we should look at as a historical anomaly? Is that the exception or the rule for the work of the Church today?

I maintain that is the rule and not the exception. I have already addressed that growth and increase are confirming signs that God is with any church. Lack of growth and increase are unacceptable (more on that in the Appendix). If there is no increase, then we must at least ask, "Why not?" There may be very good reasons, but the question must be asked, answers sought, and solutions applied. One reason why there may not be growth is that, like David trying to wear Saul's armor, a church is trying to be like another church they admire instead of following God's plan for their own identity.

You may object at this point. *That's all well and good for your church. You're large and have plenty of resources. We are small and have limited financial and human resources.* If that is what you are thinking, then you need to change your thinking. There has never been a better day to serve the Lord. We have better transportation, better and convenient communication media, and easier access to training materials than ever before. You need to stop making excuses and start becoming a vibrant body that embodies the Holy Spirit of life and growth. As you will see in the next step, there are plenty of ways for you to impact the world and develop your own identity as an outpost of God's kingdom in the world today. Let's turn our attention to that Seventh Step in the next chapter.

CHAPTER 9
QUESTIONS FOR DISCUSSION OR STUDY

1. How do you define creativity? Is it a thought or idea no

one has ever had, or can it be creatively applying or combining what already exists? Consider bottled water. The inventors didn't invent the bottle or water; they just creatively combined the two.

2. Do you agree that the church should be a creative machine, so to speak? Why do you think it has not been more creative?

3. Who are your creative heroes? Who are those who stimulate your creativity? Does your church pursue creative solutions to common problems, both in and outside the church?

4. Do you believe the book of Acts represents the church as it should be, or presents a model of what the church could be?

5. What steps can you take to stimulate and develop your creativity?

6. Where have you copied something or someone without thinking it through to make it part of who you are? Has your church done that?

7. What dead rituals does your church maintain? Do you have any personal ones? You say you don't have any? Consider perfectionism. It can be a ritual if you refuse to produce, try, or show anyone anything you are working on until it is just right.

8. Go back and read Proverbs 8:22-36. Does that sound like the Lord Jesus speaking? Now read Colossians 2:2-3. What does it say about Jesus there? It seems God hides wisdom so we must seek it. Are you seeking creative wisdom? Do you believe you can receive it? If so, what evidence is in your life that you are receiving and applying it? How about in the life of your church? Is it there?

A LITTLE GOES
A LONG WAY

REFORMATION STEP SEVEN
ADDRESS AND MEET THE NEEDS OF
THE POOR, ETHNIC MINORITIES,
AND WOMEN AROUND THE WORLD.

The 2014 survey by *Christianity Today* revealed that churches with less than 200 in weekly worship attendance had an average budget of $219,370 with a median of $173,370. For those with 200-499 worshippers, an average budget of $675,290 and a median of $628,720 was reported. The percent of that income going to staff is 47%, buildings, utilities, and maintenance 22%, program expenses received 10%, and missions was last at 5%.[8]

I am not questioning any church's need for facilities or staff. I am simply raising the question of priorities as we examine the figures in the first paragraph. Should facility budgets exceed missions' budgets? Is almost 50% of income going toward salaries too much—or not enough? If the Great Commission found in Matthew 28:19-20 is truly great, then should we not expend more than we are in the needs of the world, including the needs in our own backyard neighborhoods?

> "Therefore go and make disciples of all nations, baptizing them in the name of the Father and of the Son and of the Holy Spirit, and teaching them to obey everything I have commanded you. And surely I am with you always, to the very end of the age" (Matthew 28:19-20).

In my travels, I have seen poverty like I have never seen in the United States, and it moves me deeply. Yet I was stuck in an American mindset that big is better and because what I could do was not very large or significant, I chose to do nothing at all. Because I could not give $1,000, I didn't give $100, I did not give $10; and because I could not give $10—well, you get the idea.

Churches and their leaders may have the same thinking. Therefore, we don't do what we can because we are stuck in our own little world, judging the needs of those outside the U.S. based on our own understanding of what it takes to make a difference "out there." Meanwhile, wars, famines, droughts, genocide, and political oppression bring untold suffering to millions every year and the church doesn't do anything because it considers what it could do as insignificant. What James wrote still remains true today:

> Religion that God our Father accepts as pure and faultless is this: to look after orphans and widows in their distress and to keep oneself from being polluted by the world (James 1:27).

What more can we do to embrace this seventh step? I

don't think it's just a matter of trying to give away more from what we already have. There are, however, some practical steps we can take to increase our income so we can then increase missions giving for the gospel and the poor. Here are some thoughts.

1. More teaching on the subject to educate people that they do not have to participate in the consumer race to obtain more, better, and newer material possessions. The pandemic of 2020 has taught people they can live with less while also reinforcing what they cannot live without: family, relationships, and kindness.

2. More teaching about sacrificial giving, which is then modeled in the church by leaders who don't always drive the best car or live in the nicest home. What if everyone in a church was challenged to lower their cable or telephones bills by 10% and then to give the savings to missions?

3. Providing creative ideas of how people can increase giving, not for buildings or projects, but for needs in the world. I am convinced many people, as well as churches, have things they have not used in a year or more. Those items are prime targets to sell or to give away to someone who needs them. I have seen people who had "nothing," or so they thought, raise two hundred dollars from a garage sale. I have seen others use their talents to bake cookies and sell them to family, friends, or at their workplace, also for hundreds of dollars.

4. Step Three involved helping people incorporate their own nonprofit organizations to help finance ministries and missions passions. Some people and organizations will not give to churches but will give

to individuals whom they know and trust. That is why we need to encourage people to start their own ministries and nonprofits. Remember, the church is supposed to empower members for the work of ministry.

5. By sponsoring more short-term missions trips, or publicizing those sponsored by other reputable organizations, people will have a chance to go and see for themselves what life is like in other parts of the world. They usually come home more ready to share with others, both at home and abroad. I have told audiences I don't think anyone's salvation experience is complete until they have a passport. Otherwise, when that person says, "God, I'll go wherever You want," they are being less than honest, for they cannot go out of the country on short notice. Many told me that they could not get off work to apply, so I called the U.S. Passport Service and invited them to come to the church where I was working. They agreed and set up a processing center right in the church lobby. In two days, they processed seventy-five applications.

You may think, "Wait a minute, shouldn't we take the money we would spend on those trips and invest that in missions?" While that is a good idea, the problem is most people will not give to someone for a cause like they will to fund a trip. The money invested in a trip can be seen as an investment and money raised for causes once people return as a return on that investment. That is why we must help people raise money once they come home, capitalizing on their enthusiasm and motivation to alleviate the suffering they saw firsthand.

6. Help people realize the little they can do can truly go a long way.

7. If nothing else, perhaps just a refresher review of what the Bible has to say about the poor would be all it takes to get Step Seven activated in any church. Here are some passages to consider just from the book of Proverbs, the book of wisdom about helping the poor (it must be a wise thing to recognize and then try to meet the needs of the poor).

   • He who oppresses the poor shows contempt for their Maker, but whoever is kind to the needy honors God (Proverbs 14:31).

   • A poor man pleads for mercy, but a rich man answers harshly (Proverbs 18:23).

   • He who is kind to the poor lends to the Lord, and He will reward him for what he has done (Proverbs 19:17).

   • If a man shuts his ears to the cry of the poor, he too will cry out and not be answered (Proverbs 21:13).

   • Rich and poor have this in common: The Lord is the Maker of them all (Proverbs 22:2).

   • A generous man will himself be blessed, for he shares his food with the poor (Proverbs 22:9).

   • He who oppresses the poor to increase his wealth and he who gives gifts to the rich—both come to poverty (Proverbs 22:16).

   • Do not exploit the poor because they are poor and do not crush the needy in court (Proverbs 22:22).

   • He who increases his wealth by exorbitant interest amasses it for another, who will be kind to the poor (Proverbs 28:8).

- He who gives to the poor will lack nothing, but he who closes his eyes to them receives many curses (Proverbs 28:27).

- The righteous care about justice for the poor, but the wicked have no such concern (Proverbs 29:7).

- The poor man and the oppressor have this in common: The Lord gives sight to the eyes of both (Proverbs 29:13).

- If a king judges the poor with fairness, his throne will always be secure (Proverbs 29:14).

The best response to this step isn't necessarily for churches to give more from the money they have or receive in their weekly offering. The key is to empower the people in the church to do more. That may mean fewer special offerings and some changes in church budgeting, including building a little less or some things not at all, while making do with what we have. I have seen my friends in Africa build large functional church buildings with very little in the way of furnishings or decorations. They are content to have a place to meet, even if it isn't the prettiest or most comfortable.

I know we can do more with less, but I am not even calling for that to happen. I am appealing to churches to raise the awareness of the needs in the world and trust the Spirit to lead the people, including our youth, to embrace and fulfill their role in meeting those needs. Here are two examples from my life.

A number of years ago, I was watching a news show, and they had a report on Afghanistan about the effect the ruling Taliban was having on women in that country. I watched and listened in horror, and I did something I don't often do—I cried! Then I prayed and said, "Lord, if you need someone to go there at some point, I will be glad to go." Five years later

I received an invitation to go, and my church helped make it happen (but did not pay for my entire trip; they just encouraged me with a gift toward the $5,000 cost of the excursion). That trip changed my life, and I refer back to the lessons I learned on that trip again and again.

About ten years ago, it occurred to me that I have been to Africa many times and taken much home with me in the way of finances, encouragement, and purpose. I felt I was not doing enough to put something back in (although I always tried to leave a good deposit through my work and teaching). Consequently, I began to raise money for what I called The Sophia Fund, named in memory of my late mother who always seemed to be feeding people. The money was designated for feeding widows and orphans, with no overhead taken out of contributions whatsoever. I accepted the money through my nonprofit, PurposeQuest International.

As I write, I have raised in excess of $250,000. Then I began to collect books and send them over to Kenya to start libraries and have taken on the support for many orphans. I didn't go running to my church to do all that. I did it, and I am no one special. Therefore, if we equip other people to believe they can do the same, they will collect money from people their churches may never touch.

These two stories are a microcosm of what I see as the essence of Step Seven. I know stories like mine can happen with thousands of believers. The Church must give people a vision so they see and understand the world's needs and then equip them so they can make a difference. Members need to understand their role in church is not to sit and listen to others who are making an impact but to make an impact themselves.

If they cannot give money, and many can't, then they can give themselves, their time, and their prayers. Some can serve on governing boards and offer their life's wisdom and expertise to those who are making an impact. Others can offer their creativity that could lead to some significant idea or a breakthrough for the poor or unreached.

There you have the Seven Steps I am recommending for purposeful church reformation in this early part of the twenty-first century. These Seven Steps were part of my original edition, and in the next section, I will present my newest, eighth step. These seven may seem radical and rooted in idealism, but I am convinced these principles have the power to change the way we do church as we know it. By way of review, let's look at the Seven Steps one more time.

THE SEVEN STEPS TO CHURCH REFORMATION

1. Raise up an army of purpose-led men and women who have faith to do the impossible, freed from trying to be who they are not and released to be the fullest, best expression of who God created them to be.

2. Equip people to perform missions (both domestic and foreign), to launch business ventures, and to carry out any other activity their purpose dictates and faith allows.

3. Help leaders be productive in their purpose as they oversee the Holy Spirit chaos created by people pursuing and fulfilling their purpose.

4. Help leaders and governing bodies move from attitudes of ownership to attitudes of servant leadership and stewardship.

5. Develop services, Sunday Schools, kid's church, youth meetings, and even committee meetings that people want to attend because they involve a spirit of excellence and the unexpected.

6. Move from fads, copycat programs, and trite and phony rituals, traditions, and doctrines to innovative initiatives in the Spirit of (but exceeding the results of) the early church.

7. Address and meet the needs of the poor, ethnic minorities, and women around the world.

You may read those Seven Steps and not know where to start. I can understand, and I don't want to leave you hanging. The next chapter includes more practical suggestions of how you and your church can get started applying the principles outlined in these Seven Steps.

CHAPTER 10
QUESTIONS FOR DISCUSSION OR STUDY

1. What are you doing for the poor? How can you do more?

2. What is your church doing for the poor? Do you know? How can the church do more?

3. Are you afraid to talk about money in a church setting? Do you talk about it too much? How have past scandals affected your ability to think or talk about giving?

4. Read Philippians 4:10-20. What did Paul teach about giving in that passage? Why did he want people to give? Was Paul the direct recipient of any of the giving? Was it forced giving, or were the Philippians freely giving?

5. Read Luke 21:1-4. Who was watching when the woman gave? Who is watching when we give today? Was her giving evaluated by what she gave or what she had left after she gave?

6. Where have you *not* done anything because you could not do everything? Where have you not given a little because you could not give a lot?

7. Which one of the Seven Steps impacted you the most? Why do you think that is?

8. What personal changes will you make as a result of the Seven Steps?

9. What church changes will you initiate to apply one or more of the Seven Steps?

10. How aware are you of the plight of women and children

around the world? In your own nation? In your own city or neighborhood?

11. Read Proverbs 21:13. How do you think not caring for the poor can affect your prayer life or the prayer life of your church?

BABY STEPS FOR
THE SEVEN STEPS

I have outlined a seven-step plan to help reform the modern church of Jesus Christ so that she can become a more purposeful, productive entity. The Seven Steps are designed to accomplish three results:

1. Put leaders more in touch with the purpose of the members.

2. Put the members more in touch with their role in the body of Christ.

3. Allow the church to be purpose-driven, mission-driven, bold, and outward-focused.

All these steps will require leaders to develop new styles and skills to be more effective servant leaders. These steps will also require that members no longer be content with being spectators in the work of the church. It demands that churches make room for various callings and gifts beyond the traditional roles of church work like ushers, choir, and nursery.

These Seven Steps are lofty ideals for any group or individual to pursue and require that leaders and followers develop greater capacity and skill than is currently present in many churches. To get where we need to go, I would like to recommend three basic steps you can take to help the Seven Steps take hold and gain momentum.

1. APPOINT A PURPOSE PASTOR

Someone at a staff or leadership level needs to become the purpose champion for your church. This would involve someone who would become thoroughly immersed in purpose principles and be available to help people better understand how to find and fulfill their purpose. This person would then help people strategize their way toward fulfilling their purpose.

When I was on staff at my church from 2009 to 2014, my title was Administrative Pastor for Discipleship and decided to serve as a purpose pastor without a title or even making an announcement to that effect. I mentioned some of the things I did in chapter nine, which were:

1. Held quarterly purpose seminars that were free and open to the public. They were four hours in length and covered purpose, personality profiles, spiritual gifts, strengths and weaknesses, and creativity.

2. To help me facilitate those seminars, I recruited people to what I called the Divine Design Team. We meet regularly to talk about purpose and how we could promote it in the congregation. Then they attended the seminars and sat at a table to facilitate questions and discussions. Each member was then available to meet with others

one on one to help them apply what they had learned from the seminar.

Because I was the lead teacher in the purpose seminars as well as a pastor, most people who wanted a follow up session after the seminars requested one with me. In the five years on staff, I met with about 350 people one-on-one. I saw many people get involved in the church after our meetings, and their involvement was much more in line with who they were and what God had created them to do. I helped about six people start their own nonprofit organizations because I knew their purpose would not fit into the church's structure.

In my mind, this is what purpose pastors should achieve on a regular basis. While they are helping the people with purpose, the purpose pastors are also helping leadership understand the church's role and responsibilities in helping people find and fulfill purpose. Consequently, the purpose pastors would also be the ones to coordinate the children's book seminar I recommended the church sponsor (see chapter five). In short, the purpose pastor would be responsible to help people and the church recognize and act upon whatever emerges as the Spirit moves among the people or the leadership regarding purpose and outreach. There is more on the role of a purpose pastor in the next section.

2. A LIFE PURPOSE CENTER

I hope that a Life Purpose Center (LPC) springs up in every church serious about applying the Seven Steps. This Center will be a place where people, church leadership, and people governing organizations are trained in the principles of purpose and productivity. The LPC will have plenty of resources available to help people no matter what level of purpose search. The purpose pastor may be the director of the LPC or leadership can come from someone else who works closely with the purpose pastor.

The LPC will conduct regular seminars for leaders to train and equip them to be more effective servant leaders. Resources and training for skills such as listening, consensus building, and facilitating will also be available. Leaders can find coaches to help them with those key skill areas at the LPC, or they can just come to an LPC for personal reflection, to read leadership books in the library, or to watch video presentations that pertain to leadership development.

Members will come to the LPC for coaching and mentoring as well. They can attend regular workshops on time management, creativity, starting businesses and non-profit organizations, writing, website design, and other Internet media development. A host of personality profiling and other assessment tools can also be available that will help people better understand who they are and who they are not, with someone available to explain the results while helping them develop plans for growth and improvement.

Members will also come and watch or listen to self-help training and equipping programs. There will be a library of purpose, theology, and leadership books. There will be reading groups formed to study various topics or to develop specific skills among those attending. There will be writing support groups that meet regularly to encourage one another in creative development. Assistance with publishing of personal works will also be available, and regular art exhibits will be held to encourage emerging artists. Obviously, many of these resources can be online for people to access anytime they wish. Again, there will be more on this in the next section.

The emphasis will not simply be on creativity, but on whatever emphasis happens to "bubble up" from the people. For example, if there is a need for business expertise, business experts will be brought in to work with the people. Of course, there will be a special emphasis on youth, and young people can come to get a full understanding of what their purpose is and how to express it now and in the future. Every effort will be made to help them prepare for purpose and not short-circuit their purpose in the interests of short-term monetary gain by taking a job not suited to who God made them to be.

There is no end to the possibilities for an LPC that is closely tied to the life of a local church, network of churches, fellowship, or denomination. There will of course be Internet resources available from the LPC, which can be accessed by people anywhere in the world, thus making LPC a source of missionary outreach on a 24/7 basis. I could go on and on about the possibilities, but I think you get the point. Every LPC will be unique according to the vision of the church and the needs of the people, but each one will have the same objective: equip people and leaders to embrace the Seven Steps to purposeful church reformation. Again, more on this in the next section.

3. A LEADERSHIP DEVELOPMENT PROGRAM

I read once that eighty percent of a leader's time should be spent developing the leader within that leader. I don't know if the percentage is correct, but I do know leaders need to spend a lot of time fine-tuning and honing their leadership skills. What's more, church leaders need to have a program where they are also directly involved training the people among whom they serve. Jack Welch, former CEO of GE Corporation, spent thirty-three percent of his work time at GE's training center working with and training leaders in mandatory sessions. During these sessions, management could ask him anything they wanted about GE and its direction and decisions. If Jack Welch could spend that much time in training, how much should church leaders invest in the same?

There was a day when leaders were developed in the Church and sent out into the world with a solid Christian worldview and biblical foundation. Today, the opposite is true. Most leaders are shaped in the world and then they come to church. This is sometimes even true for those who come to lead the church. I am not implying that someone who learned good business principles should not apply them to church management. I am saying the philosophy of servant leadership is not prevalent in the church because the leadership philosophies being taught to leaders today are either trite (the case for most church teachings) or secular (the context for humanist theories).

The changed church that wants to see any of the Seven Steps addressed and achieved will need a new leadership, as mentioned earlier in this book, for that to happen. That is why I am recommending a leadership training program in churches and seminaries that imparts the skills and thinking necessary for a purposeful reformation the Church so desperately needs.

Wherever I have been a pastor or elder, I have pushed for a mandatory training policy or program that involved regular classes and one annual conference to which staff would go to enhance their skills. (The church would pay some or all of the expenses whenever possible.) The church also agreed to pay half of any Bible school or university courses that were related to the area in which the staff person served. This, however, should only be one part of any leadership development program.

Each employee should have a personalized development program toward which that individual works. That may mean a degree or advanced degree. It could be a certification in some special program or skill. Every senior leader, elder, staff person, and significant volunteer should develop such a personalized plan. Every five years a leader at any level should be given a three-month study sabbatical, during which time they would do something consistent with and contributing toward their educational and development goals. There should also be a mandatory international missions trip that each leader must take every three to five years.

Additionally, the leadership of the church, working

with the purpose pastor and LDC, would work diligently to recognize potential leaders in their midst, especially among the youth. Plans and opportunities for these potential leaders could be developed so the church would always be working to develop leaders from within the church. Those potential leaders may serve the church in the future or go on to express their leadership in another sphere of life such as education, the military, government, or business. Either way, the church "wins" as a steady stream of qualified leaders is available to the church or society at large.

REFORMATION

As stated earlier, if we want what we have never had, we must begin to do what we have never done. That is the essence of reformation. Reformation, however, is a heart matter and not just about techniques and programs. If there isn't a desire for reform, then those in favor of reform will be at odds with those who like things just the way they are.

I argue, however, that things cannot stay the way they are in the church for much longer without even more damage being done. As I wrote the first edition, I was on my way home from a trip abroad where I heard countless horror stories of the misdeeds and lack of integrity on the part of church leaders and church "celebrities" whose names you would recognize if I mentioned them—many of them American, but not all. Now as I write the second edition, the world is in the grip of a pandemic that has forced churches to alter the way they deliver ministry. We need to change the way we do church in 2020 even more so than when I wrote this book in 2009.

I still believe in the Church. I know Jesus gave His life to build the church, and I am called to be a leader in that church. I must not withhold my gifts or perspective if it can help it grow and be more effective to reach more people. I am not nailing these Eight Steps to any church door like Luther, demanding another reformation. I am not moving to another city like Calvin did to try and build a utopian community. I am willing to work with what we have and who we are, as imperfect as we all are (including me).

There you have my plan. I hope it will promote dialogue and that you will write me with your ideas, comments, and criticisms of the Seven Steps—and still have the courage to move on the eighth step in the next section. More importantly, I hope you will apply some of what you read to your own world. If you are a leader, you have a great opportunity to make a difference in the lives of many people. Who knows, God may give you a broad platform beyond your own world to impact many people.

If you are a follower, you don't have to wait for anyone else to embrace these steps for reformation. The most important thing you can do is to become a person of purpose. Then determine to express your purpose, even if no one comes along to help you. God will assist you, and you plus God always make a majority. If God be for you, who can be against you? Grow strong, build yourself up, and keep on doing so. God does not promote potential; He promotes people who have developed their potential. You can do that without anyone's permission or help, if need be.

My contact information is at the end of this book, so please write when you can. Let me know your success stories and send your questions. Together we can make a difference. Will you stand up and be counted in this hour of critical need? If so, I hope this book will help you be a purposeful reformer in your world and work. And I hope you will move on to read what I have to say about Step Eight in Section Three that involves the effective use of social media and technology.

CHAPTER 11
QUESTIONS FOR DISCUSSION OR STUDY

1. Does the concept of a Purpose Pastor make sense to you?

Is there anyone you know who seems gifted at recognizing the potential or purpose in others? Do you know anyone who is gifted at listening and then helping others strategize the way forward? That is the kind of person who would make a good Purpose Pastor.

2. What are you doing to grow in the awareness of who you are and how you function best?

3. What plan does your church have to recognize talent, giftedness, or purpose? How often is this discussed in your leadership meetings?

4. What simple steps could you take to open a Life Purpose Center? What are some of the steps you could take to make the Center effective? (One of the things I did was pay to develop my mobile app where I could put all my training and teaching videos and connect people to my world.)

5. What is your church's leadership development plan to equip new and existing leaders?

6. Leaders are readers. What are you reading? What books do you want to read? Does your church promote reading and learning? How can they do that more effectively?

7. If you were in charge of the LPC, what would you do for the first year?

8. If you were given responsibility for your church's leadership development plan, what would your first year's plan be? What training would you offer for whom?

9. Since you are responsible for your own personal development, what is your plan for the next year? The next two years? Five years?

ENDNOTES FOR SECTIONS ONE AND TWO

1 Robert K. Greenleaf, *Servant Leadership* (New York: Paulist Press, 1977), page 13.

2 Larry C. Spear, editor, *Insights on Leadership* (New York: John Wiley and Sons, Inc., 1998), page 23.

3 *Ibid.*, page 25.

4 Robert K. Greenleaf, *On Becoming a Servant-Leader* (San Francisco: Jossey-Bass Publishers, 1996), page 129.

5 *Ibid.*

6 *Ibid.*, page 140.

7 Marcus Buckingham and Curt Coffman, *First, Break All the Rules* (New York: Simon and Schuster, 1999), pages 56-57.

8. https://www.pnwumc.org/news/how-churches-spend-their-money/

SECTION THREE

ADDED IN 2020

STEP EIGHT:

UTILIZE TECHNOLOGY AND SOCIAL MEDIA
NOT AS AN AFTERTHOUGHT OR SIDE SHOW
BUT RATHER AS SOMETHING EQUAL IN
IMPORTANCE TO FACE-TO-FACE MINISTRY.

WHY THIS
NEW SECTION?

In 1987, Stephen Covey wrote his classic best-selling book, *The 7 Habits of Highly Effective People*, which had 372 pages in the soft cover version. Then in 2004 he published *The 8ᵗʰ Habit: From Effectiveness to Greatness*, which was a book about purpose, and the eighth habit being "find your voice and help others find theirs." That hardback book had 378 pages. My point is that his eighth habit had as many pages as all seven of his previous habits. I promise this section is not the same size as what you have already read—but it's close.

It is hard to imagine a book that focused on changing the way we do church not including a section on technology. When I first wrote this book in 2009, I was a novice to Facebook. I had been using it for only three years and had been blogging for about that long as well. I don't recall if I was using Twitter, but Instagram, Snapchat, the cloud, smartphones, and iPads were just coming into their own. A church was considered cutting-edge in 2009 if it was able to put their Sunday service online using their own website; social media wasn't yet a possibility as a means to do so.

Now in 2020, we have an explosion of social media options and opportunities, and quite frankly, most of the Church is stuck, utilizing little if any of the available options. Some churches livestream their services and maintain them in an archive for future reference. Some have blogs, chat rooms for prayer and counseling, and actively publish other ministry resources.

Yet many churches are yet to even make the transition to the digital age. Those churches don't have websites, do not pay much attention to social media, and are addicted to what I call face-to-face ministry. Unless someone comes in the door of the church, there is no relationship or attempt to establish one, nor is there a belief that meaningful ministry can happen apart from personal encounters.

Lo and behold, in 2020 we have a world crisis known as the COVID-19 virus pandemic. The entire world was sent home, including the Church, and everyone, including the Church, had one thing to utilize to stay in touch: social media through technology! We had gas in our tanks and clothes in our closets but nowhere to go, so we either watched television, read a book, or learned how to utilize things like Zoom, Facebook, GoToMeeting, LinkedIn, or for some, the features of a smartphone.

Many leaders I talk to are ambivalent or downright hostile toward the concept of anything but face-to-face ministry—and it has showed up in their demeanor or words when using social media. I have watched many church "broadcasts" on Facebook during this time of sheltering in place, and it is clear they are uncomfortable and ready to go back to "normal" as soon as the all-clear alarm is sounded. Most have simply tried to replicate their live services online without anyone monitoring who may be watching, if those watching have any prayer needs, or if those watching are "visitors" to the online service. That tells me their online presence is a stopgap measure that is not being considered as a permanent feature or fixture in the church's ministry repertoire.

Why does my generation hate social media like many do? When I pose that question, I hear the usual complaints:

- "Those who use social media are self-absorbed."

- "I don't have time for anything but preparing my Sunday message and caring for the needs of those in the church."

- "If we deploy social media, people will stay home and not attend church."

- "People need to stop playing with their phones and pay attention to one another."

- "We don't have money for technology."

- "We have no interest in broadcasting what we do to the larger public. Our first responsibility is to take care of our own."

- "Social media destroys relationships, and the Church is all about relationships. We must have face-to-face time to build and cultivate relationships."

I am sure you can add other laments to the list—those you have heard or uttered yourself.

Before the pandemic, the ministry opportunities available through the creative use of social media were huge—and now they are even greater. For example, one-sixth of the world's population is now on Facebook. The Church was given the Great Commission to go into all the world, so now we can simply go to our computer (or phone) to reach a large portion of it. When we "go," we have access to do or say pretty much anything we want and people are free to read or not, respond or not, reflect or not. *What would happen if we paid as much attention to our online presence as we did to our in-person presence?* That is the question I was asking before the pandemic.

The new, more relevant questions are now, *What will happen if we **don't** pay as much attention to our online presence? What is going to happen to our church financial model? How will we fund ministry? Will people stay home after the pandemic? Will our content be censored, hacked, edited, or misused? What will happen to those who are currently addicted to face-to-face ministry if we don't open up the church? Will they go to another church?*

All these are real concerns, and I am not here to predict what will happen. All I am saying is the shift to technology which was optional before the pandemic is mandatory now. Before COVID-19, Church attendance was down; now it's almost nonexistent. People don't like change and shifting to a broader, more strategic use of technology is a *big* change. For some, attending a church service anchored their week; for others it was a ritual. What will happen when the all-clear signal is given? Will people continue to rely on social media, apprehensive to assemble for fear of a new wave of sickness?

My own sense is that this represents a significant opportunity for the Church to do what it should have been doing through the appropriate and aggressive use of technology. God is using this pandemic, as He has other past plagues, famines, and catastrophes, to awaken and reposition His people for more effective ministry and witness.

I once attended a meeting for a few discipleship pastors from large churches. I was touting the benefits of using technology for training, testimonies, and all kinds of discipleship practices that were not new, but were usually delivered in the traditional ways. There was another pastor there who was half my age who kept dismissing what I said: "We don't need to use any technology. We need to get people to be with one another so they can learn how to talk again!" This went on for three days.

As we wrapped up our time, one of the other pastors who was closer to my age than my "opponent" said this pointing to me, "You talk like I would have thought our young friend would talk, and he talks like I would have expected you to talk." In other words, he was surprised someone in his sixties (back then) would be such a proponent of technology in the Church. Perhaps it would be helpful if I shared with you in the next chapter how I came to use social media as I do that has led to the recommendations I am making in this section. Before we get there, however, let me keep the same format I had in the first two sections by providing some questions for thought and discussion.

CHAPTER 12
QUESTIONS FOR DISCUSSION OR STUDY

1. What is your attitude toward social media? If you are in church leadership, what is the attitude of your church?

2. What is your philosophy for social media usage? If you are in church leadership, what is the usage of your church?

3. Is there any benefit to using social media as I have described in this chapter? What are the drawbacks in your estimation?

4. Do you agree that the Church in general has been slow to adopt technology as a means to enhance discipleship? If so, is this warranted? Why or why not?

5. What was your experience with social media during the pandemic? Did it make any difference in how you will utilize technology going forward? What are those changes?

MY SOCIAL MEDIA
JOURNEY

You can label me an early adopter of social media and technology with 20 years of experience as I write. I had no choice but to make the shift to technology when in 2001, I had my own ministry pandemic. I was suddenly isolated and quarantined from all my ministry relationships because of a decision I made to leave a church and move on to fulfill my own ministry. When I left that church, I lost everything—friends, ministry opportunities, finances, and identity—and almost lost my sanity. At the age of 51, what was I to do? I had no one to call for help, but I knew I had a message on life purpose that had begun to reach people where they lived.

My first thought was to start a website, but what good would that do? People would look at it once and then forget about it, unless they had some incentive or reminder to go there again and again. Then I read a book by Seth Godin that talked about permission marketing. The goal, he explained, was not to interrupt and intercept people's attention, but to build relationships with potential online readers who would welcome, or at least not mind, if I sent them regular updates. They had given me permission to do so. More on that later.

My idea was to start writing what I called the *Monday Memo* that would focus on the topic of purpose and faith every week. Since many people had told me over the years, "We love your message, but we need more help to understand what our purpose is." I figured if I wrote people every week—sending it to people who wanted to hear from me and gave me permission to send an email—then I could promote my website, sell books, and further the cause of my purpose message, all at the same time.

The *Monday Memo* started going out to eight people who enrolled after I conducted a workshop in Ohio, but it quickly grew. When I finally got my website up and running, it worked as I had hoped—to an extent. By showing up every week, I gave people a reason to visit my website, although I didn't sell any books. People were eager to get the free stuff from my site, but they were in no hurry to purchase books or coaching services—or to contribute to my ministry.

As I traveled to Africa, Asia, and the UK, people kept enrolling for the *Memo*, and I managed it all using my Outlook email service. I had a glimpse of the power of online connections to raise money when I expressed a need for ministry funds to travel to Afghanistan, as I described earlier. People gave almost $5,000 for the trip, but before and after that, I had little success—and I was desperate for income. Well-meaning people would tell me, "You have 2,000 subscribers. You just need to get them to pay you $1 every month and you will have a nice stream of income." The problem was that I could not get *some* of the people to give $1 per month, let alone all of them.

I handed out cards wherever and whenever I spoke, and people gave me their name and email address with permission to enroll them to receive the *Memo*. I would then go into my Outlook account and put their information in a distribution list with a name, like Kenya 1, Kenya 2, Zimbabwe 1, Zimbabwe 2, etc. After I had about 50 names in a list, I would start a new one. Then when I wrote a *Memo*, I would copy and paste it so I could send that *Memo* to each distribution list.

After a few years, I had about 18,000 names in Outlook (I entered every one of them myself) and was copying and pasting the *Monday Memo* many times every week. When someone wrote to "unsubscribe," I had to go through all my lists to find their email address. Because I am a glutton for punishment, I started a weekly online Bible study that followed the same pattern, and eventually I had 6,000 names receiving that study—and went through the same cut-and-paste procedure for that.

God was merciful and eventually put me out of my weekly Outlook misery. I had so many names in my account that it crashed. Clearly, I had to change my mode of delivery. After a few months of not sending out a *Memo*, a reader wrote to suggest I convert the *Memo* into a blog, which was fairly new at that time. I could import all my names from Outlook into a blog service, write one *Memo* or Bible study, and all the subscribers would automatically receive it. Then the reader would be responsible to unsubscribe or change email addresses. That certainly made my life easier.

In 2006, I started a personal blog at www.johnstanko.us and began writing regularly about servant leadership, purpose, and anything else that was on my mind. That meant I then was writing for three personal blog sites. In 2009, I accepted a position at my church as pastor of discipleship and quickly realized that most of the staff had no idea who I was. I decided to send them a daily devotional via email that I adapted from my book, *A Daily Dose of Proverbs*. These entries were much shorter than those found in the book but were well received by the staff. Let me list the new programs and online services I offered after 2010:

1. After the first year of sending a daily dose of Proverbs, I

decided to post what I was sending to the staff on my personal blog for the public to see, and again people enjoyed them and missed them if I took a break. At some point, I started placing the link for this daily devotional on my Facebook page, while also including a short summary on Twitter. My friends and followers began to increase and I published them and gave it the name *A Daily Taste of Proverbs*.

2. At the end of 2011, I was tired of doing the cycle of daily proverbs, so I decided to produce a different daily online devotional. I had been "collecting" questions Jesus asked in the gospels, so I started writing a daily devotional using one of those questions as the subject focus. When I ran out of gospel questions, I went into other parts of Scripture and had enough for 366 days.

   From those, I wrote a daily devotional called *Purpose Pearls*, which focused on my five Gold Mine Principles of purpose, goals, time management, organization, and faith. In 2014, I produced an online devotional directed at leadership titled *The Leadership Walk* and in 2015, it was *Your Life Matters*, a daily devotional with verses from the book of Psalms. Every one of these daily devotionals is still online, free for the taking, but they are also available in paper and electronic book formats. Notice that my writing online became the basis for my books and not the other way around.

3. In 2012, I continued my habit of publishing my devotionals each day on Twitter and Facebook, and my 1,200 subscribers to my blog received the devotional via email the day after it was published. At some point, I added LinkedIn as a publishing source and also posted my daily devotional and *Monday Memo* on that predominantly business medium.

4. In 2014, I founded a publishing company called Urban

Press and I did so for two reasons. One was to help others know the joy of seeing their creativity come to life in the form of a book. The other was to publish or republish my own works, thus having more control and reaping more of the meager profits that are generated. Because I had access to publishing expertise through my company, I decided to publish *all* my devotionals, making sure they were available in paper and e-book formats.

5. From 2003-2009, I completed my online commentary on all 8,000 verses in the New Testament, posting each study on my website (where they remain) after I sent it to my weekly mailing list. Today, I have published those studies in a 12-volume set called *Live the Word Commentaries*. I chose that name because I want those who read my commentaries not only to study the Word but, more importantly, also apply it to their daily lives.

6. In 2017, I revised my first book, *Life is a Gold Mine*, for the third time, publishing it as a 20th-anniversary edition. I made a major revision in that edition, for I changed the five Gold Mine Principles to include creativity to go along with purpose, goals, time management (into which I merged the old Principle of organization), and faith. Along with that anniversary edition, I revised my daily devotional *String of Pearls* to include more entries on creativity and re-published it under the title *Life is a Gold Mine Daily Devotional*.

7. As I revise this book, I post a devotional from one of my five published devotional books on Facebook, LinkedIn, and Twitter every Monday through Friday. I use that opportunity to edit and update that day's entry because the files are so easy to edit with the print-on-demand format used today in publishing.

I hope you get the idea that I am heavily invested in social media and technology. It is an important part of my ministry and a lifeline to thousands around the world.

Why am I telling you all this? I am doing so because I am desperate for the Church to hear what I am saying. I am a voice crying in the wilderness, "Repent, for the Kingdom of social media is at hand." I am now raising money regularly through social media, for I finally realized why people gave to my Afghanistan trip but not to much else. People want to give to someone they know and trust who is doing something with life and purpose. I have built a following, dare I say *relationships*, over the years and people give because they know me. I have come to them almost every day, sharing my life, travels, and spiritual insights and now when I ask, they trust me. They may not give. They may not ever read what I send, but they trust me. They may disagree with what I write or say, but they trust me.

This proves that relationships *can* be established and maintained through social media. Is it the same as face to face? Absolutely not. Can it replace existing relationships? Absolutely not. Can it replace church services? Absolutely not. Technology can, however, take the place of those things in an emergency, as we have learned during the pandemic, and those connections, if nurtured and cared for properly, can do much more than many thought possible.

For years, I had provided windows into what I was doing in Africa by writing blogs and posting pictures and videos of my travels to Africa and the Middle East. Some people took the initiative to send me financial support, but most people were content to read or watch and enjoy—but not give. Finally, I became more proactive and *asked* for help, and gave people a chance to give through PayPal, Facebook, the mail, and now through my mobile app (nore on that later). I am glad to report my efforts are paying off and more money was donated in 2019 and 2020 than ever before. I also promoted my trips to Israel and Kenya in 2018 via social media and had my biggest turnout ever for both trips.

That sums up my written aspect of social media, but there's more. Let's move on to see what I have done in the digital video and audio aspects of social media. Keep in mind that my reason for sharing this is to stimulate, challenge, and equip believers to change the way we do church through the use of technology and social media. Let's move on after our questions.

CHAPTER 13
QUESTIONS FOR DISCUSSION OR STUDY

1. Which social media that involve reading and writing do you prefer? Which ones are preferred at your church?

2. How do you use your social media? Do you read only? Write occasionally? What do you write about?

3. How could you more effectively use social media in your personal ministry? How could your church use it more effectively in their public ministry?

4. List all the reasons why you think you or your church or ministry don't utilize technology more than you currently do.

CHRISTIAN MEDIA

Over the years, I had more than a few opportunities to be a guest on both radio and television shows. They were usually Christian stations and would involve talking about life purpose or promoting a ministry project, sometimes for myself or for other organizations. I have more than a few humorous but also sad stories concerning Christian media and my involvement.

Once when I was a pastor, I accepted an invitation to travel to a TV station two hours from my home to speak about a ministry in South America I was serving. After I got there, they put on my makeup and I waited almost two hours to be a guest, since I was the last one to be interviewed. As the host mentioned me before we went to a station break, I noticed that he mispronounced the name of the ministry I was there to discuss, which included someone's Spanish name. I thought for sure he would want to know so he could pronounce it correctly, and therefore shared with him the correct pronunciation during the break. I was wrong.

When we went back to live, I quickly realized he was offended I had corrected him—even though I had done so in private off the air in a matter-of-fact manner. His introduction

125

of me went like this, "Well, here is John Stanko who just informed me that I have said the ministry name he represents one way, but it is to be another way," and then he refused to mention the ministry's name! I was shocked and, needless to say, the interview did not go well. I drove home and realized I had invested six hours of my day and paid for my own fuel, and did not even receive a thank you, only indignation that I had dared to correct the host (who was the founder of the station).

Then on another occasion, I was invited to be a guest on a local Christian station to discuss a water-well project in Kenya. I was on the show along with the Kenyan founder and once again, I was the last guest on the show. When it came our time to be interviewed, the host spent our entire session talking his experience in Haiti drilling wells. We never got to talk about the Kenyan project!

To be fair, I have had some powerful and moving experiences as well. Once I was preparing to be on a radio show to talk about a university program for which I was an instructor. I was to be on for 15 minutes to talk about the school, but as we went on the air, the host changed direction and said, "I am looking at your purpose website and I want to ask you a question: How would you define success?"

I was taken aback but quickly recovered to say, "I would define it as being able to do what you love and brings you joy as often as possible." No sooner had I said that when the lights on the host's call-in phone bank lit up and I was on the show for an hour, never talking about the university program, but answering people's questions and hearing their comments about what I had said. I received calls at my office for two weeks after that show, listening to people's feedback. Of course, that host promised he would have me back again soon, but the follow up invitation never came.

Then on another occasion, I was in Kenya and had a

thirty-minute time slot to talk about purpose and my ministry. My host began asking questions and once again, the phone bank lit up and I ended up being on the show for two hours. What's more, I was invited back every day for five days straight. I added 1,200 names to my *Monday Memo* Outlook lists during those five days, and I have followed that host as she has moved from station to station and invites me to be a guest to talk about purpose. All those experiences and many others showed me the power of the airwaves, but also the need for the hosts to be prepared, both spiritually and mentally. I kept waiting for more invitations to be on more shows, but they seldom came.

There could be several reasons for this. One is that my performance on their shows wasn't that good, and they were only being polite, not wanting to hurt my feelings. The feedback from those who watched and listened to the shows, however, was the same as that of the hosts. People thought the show was good, even great.

Another possibility was that I was too good, threatening the host who wanted someone who would talk less so the host could talk more. Or maybe the hosts were good talkers themselves but poor in the follow through, so they would forget or have no further use for the topics I represented. Whatever the reason, and it could be a combination of all the options and some I have not even considered, I seldom got invited back.

BLOG RADIO

Then in 2009, I heard about a concept called blog radio where I could enroll online with a service that would help me set up my own radio show without a studio. I could upload my show intro and close, call a toll-free number, have my guests call a different number, interview them, control the show with a web-based control panel, and have people call in to ask questions or make comments. All the shows would be archived so people could listen at any time. People could also leave comments at the site for each show or subscribe to receive notices when shows had aired. I decided to stop waiting for invitations that never came and started my own show for my church called *Ministry Beat*.

That show became quite popular (the service tracked the number of listeners and how long they listened) and people began approaching me to be on the show. If I promised to have people back on the show, I made sure I did so, and the listenership grew over the four years I served as host. At the same time, I approached a local Christian AM station and they sold me a Saturday morning, 60-minute slot for a show I called *Wake Up to Purpose*. I paid $100 a week to talk to listeners about purpose, usually having a guest on with me to talk about their quest for meaning. I discovered from both shows that I was an effective interviewer, having learned how not to do it from some of my bad experiences as a guest on others' shows.

I stopped producing blog radio shows in 2015 but early in the 2020 pandemic, I decided to start a show once again. To date, I have had thousands of listeners in 35 countries and have produced 70 shows in which I interviewed people of purpose and creativity from whom listeners could learn much to apply in their own purpose journey. Of course, I have promoted the shows through all my other social media outlets. These shows are not really radio, but are a network of podcasts, and the network provides a library of shows produced on a host of topics—not all Christian, by the way.

If this is what I could do, what could a church do that was committed to share who they are and what they know with the world? Yes, there is often no "return" in doing this *except* for the influence it would be on other people. This is consistent with what we discussed in Section One, which is the concept and practice of servant leadership.

VIDEO

As I got more involved with broadcasting, I did not want to neglect television or video because I once read that younger generations don't take anyone seriously *unless* they see them on a screen. I am not sure that's true, but I know video is a powerful medium because it allows the viewer to see body language and facial expressions along with the message, both of which are important in the communication process. With the help of the videographer at my church, I began to record a monthly 60-minute show called *Your PurposeQuest* for our community cable television station.

Like I did on blog radio, I hosted people I knew who had an inspiring story of how they found or fulfilled their purpose, while also promoting my books, travels, or relief work in Africa. Once the show aired, we would then post it on my personal Vimeo channel. After a while, we stopped doing the community show, but kept recording shorter shows, still posting them to Vimeo. I would also post those videos or a link to their Vimeo location on all my social media outlets: Twitter, Facebook (by then I had four separate pages), and LinkedIn.

During the pandemic, I launched a free mobile app people can download so they receive notices whenever I develop new ministry resources. One of the highlights of the app is the collection of videos I have produced on leadership, creativity, and the five Gold Mine Principles. They are high quality and are impacting and equipping people all over the world. I also took some of the sermons I preached that were on video and made them available through my app as well. Thus far, I am quite pleased with the numbers of those downloading the app and accessing my resources. By the way, I pay out of my own pocket for the video production, the app maintenance, and other media through which I share the message of purpose God has given me.

PUBLISHING

Let's return to written media for a moment. In 2014, I resigned from the position I held at my church (which I still attend) so I could travel more often to Africa and start my own publishing company. I wanted others to know the joy I have of holding a completed project in their hands, so Urban Press came into being to help people finish and publish their works.

This may sound strange, but I have found that my role as an editor and publisher has taken on the role of a pastor on more than a few occasions. In a sense, I shepherd people through the writing and publishing process, which not only includes manuscript preparation but these other aspects that require encouragement, counseling, and prayer:

1. Often people are telling personal, painful stories, and as they tell them, they may relive the trauma. It's good to have a pastor to walk through with them.

2. Others are terrified of the creative process, even though they can quote with confidence, "God has not given us a spirit of fear" (see 2 Timothy 1:7). My job is to shepherd them through the fear process to victory.

3. I have found most people underestimate the spiritual power and vitality in their stories, poems, and insights, so it becomes my task to encourage them to have faith in what they have produced and its ability to touch others.

4. People sometimes come and say, "God wants me to produce this." When I ask them how long they have had "this," they have told me, "Decades." It is then incumbent on me to help them fulfill God's will for their lives.

5. Most people have no idea what to expect when they start the publishing process. Some believe they will be able to pay off their mortgage or buy a vacation home (let it be, Lord, for all of us!) and others think people will run out of their homes to buy their book, until they realize that

there are no bookstores to which people can run. I must adjust and educate their expectations so they won't be disappointed and can then publish other things—and one of those may be the big project that pays off financially.

In my own life, I had to deal with massive fear to write and publish as I do today. My first books were nothing but long book reports on what others had written. I was not confident I had anything to say so I restated what others had already said. Then my goal was to write one book every year, only to experiment with the thought, "What if my goal is to write two? three? five? more?" In 2019, I wrote six books and am on track this year to write and publish five.

My point is that I have studied and learned about the creative process. As a pastor, I am in a position to help others because I have been there myself. During the pandemic, I co-facilitated an online class on creativity that used my book *Unlocking the Power of Your Creativity* as the discussion guide for all six sessions. The impact on the lives of the 22 students was dramatic with all sharing how the class freed them to be less self-conscious as they create. In the next chapter, I will outline again the importance of churches and believers being fully engaged in social media.

CHAPTER 14
QUESTIONS FOR DISCUSSION OR STUDY

1. During the pandemic, what has your experience been with social media?

2. Do you think your attitude and use of technology will change once the pandemic diminishes?

3. What fears do you have where technology is concerned?

4. Do you have any lingering creative projects in your mind or heart on which you have not acted? Why not? What is your plan for going forward?

5. Do you have a story to tell? Have you diminished its importance in your mind so you do not have to share it?

6. When is the last time you gave a testimony?

TECHNOLOGY AND THE AMISH

You may wonder what drove me—and *driven* is the correct word—to do so much on what came to be known as social media but in the early days was simply included in the broader category of technology. The simplest answer is that I was influenced by an author and marketing guru named Seth Godin. I had to work though Seth's terminology, which was laden with words like *client, customer, marketing,* and *sales* and then adapt his principles to my faith-based world. I will attempt to paraphrase Seth's points as I understood and assimilated them into my own work and writing. The second answer was I developed what I call a theology of social media. Let me first share what I learned from Seth, and then I will share what I learned from the Bible in the next chapter.

PERMISSION MARKETING

The main concept I learned from Seth was what he referred to as *permission marketing*. I don't think he coined the term, but he talked about the concept in a book he wrote titled

Permission Marketing: Turning Strangers into Friends and Friends into Customers. Seth taught me that the opposite of permission marketing is interruption marketing. We have experienced interruption marketing when we tried to view a *YouTube* video or some other media only to be forced to watch an ad before we were able to get to what we wanted to see.

Sometimes the ad is during the video clip rather than before. That is interruption marketing. It is capturing the reader, viewer, or listener against his or her will, making them captives to a message. I don't know about you, but I mute every such ad as best I can because I consider it a violation of my personal space and did not ask for it—and don't want it.

The opposite of interruption marketing is permission marketing. When I was developing my website in 2001, I had already visited plenty of sites once only never to visit them again, unless it was to buy something or get information I needed—like a weather forecast. I did not want to invest time and money in my own site that people would view once and never return. I asked myself what I could do to draw attention to my site in a way that didn't rely on tricking people to view it. Based on what I had learned from Seth, I decided to write a weekly *Monday Memo.* The content there would be relevant and timely and would highlight things on my site that could help people who were interested in what I had to say.

When I went out to speak, I asked those present, "Who would like to receive a short, weekly email letter that will help you be more purposeful and productive?" I had small green cards and would pass them out and ask people for their name and email address. In return, I promised to send them a weekly *Memo* until they said they no longer wanted it. That was my version of permission marketing for my ministry and purpose message.

The power behind this marketing was that people have given me permission to contact them. They may not read or utilize what I sent, but they didn't feel violated or pressured to take any particular action. They made me or my organization part of their lives because they *wanted* it, and when they no longer wanted it, they could easily withdraw—easy in, easy out. They had and have the freedom to receive or not receive, to respond or not respond.

That freedom then allows the marketer or communicator to build a relationship with the permission giver—and that is where the rub usually comes in for church folk. They don't see—and sometimes refuse to see—that relationships can be built using consistent non-face-to-face communication through technology that has value to those who receive. More on that later.

Once I became a Godin devotee, I signed up to receive his daily blog updates (I gave him permission to send them although I don't read every one of them) and I have read many of his books: *Tribes: We Need You to Lead Us; The Dip: A Little Book that Teaches You When to Quit (And When to Stick); Linchpin: Are You Indispensable?; Poke the Box; We Are All Weird; This Is Marketing: You Can't be Seen Until You Learn to See*—and those are not all of them.

The fact that I have drawn so heavily from what some church goers would label a secular source demands I have more than that to make my case to use social media effectively. I need biblical evidence (and perhaps you do too) that permission marketing and social media are biblical or at least not unbiblical. In order to do that, I will present in the next chapters what I call a theology of social media. You can read more about permission marketing and my own perspective that is quite consistent with biblical principles in the Appendix.

SPIRITUALLY AMISH

The first magazine article I ever wrote was on the topic communication and was published way back in 1979. The magazine's name was *New Wine*, which contained monthly teaching on biblical topics. Its target audience was comprised of those who had a charismatic experience but were still in a traditional denomination that was or was not open to their encounter with the Spirit—thus the magazine name of *New Wine* that could not go into old wineskins.

The study I did for that article has kept me interested in communication as a topic since then, and that study was enhanced and greatly supplemented when I served as a graduate level instructor in an organizational leadership program for which communication was one of the core classes (I taught that class three or four times).

One of the statements I made in the article was, "In this age of highly technological media bombardment and of intense competition for the attention of people, Christians face a formidable, yet crucial task, both of hearing what God says and effectively communicating it to one another and to the world." We had no idea in 1979 what "media bombardment" was when we compare communication then to what it is today. We had no Internet in 1979, no social media, no cell phones, no cable TV, no email. There were only a few channels available on our television. Because of today's bombardment, some church folk and entire churches have opted out of the onslaught, choosing instead to barricade themselves behind a technological barrier and ignore the noise of the attacked.

I liken it to the example of my dear grandmother who came to the United States as a young woman to marry my grandfather in the early 1900s. She taught herself to read English, gave birth to 13 children, and woke up every morning to fire up the coal stove so she could cook for her brood. Later in life, two of her bachelor sons served 20 years in the military and came home after they retired to live in the house in which they were raised, making renovations that included installing a landline phone. Before that phone, if we needed to get in touch with my grandmother, we called her next-door neighbor who would go and fetch my grandmother, who would then walk from her home, stepping over the stream that came from the outhouse toilet, and walk about 50 yards to the neighbor's house.

The image I have of believers who have checked out of the social media culture is of my grandmother who made do with what someone else had in order to stay in touch. She was cute and old fashioned, but out of touch. In fact, if we search for an example of people who are out of touch with cultural communication norms, we have only to look a few hours from where I live to find the Amish, who have rejected all technology, including vehicles, electricity, and other modern advancements.

The Amish are cultural freaks and people travel from far and wide to see them, buy food from their farm stands, and learn of and marvel at their out-of-touch ways. Yet no one wants to become an Amish. No child comes home to say, "Mom and Dad, I have decided to convert to Amish-ism, and wear a straw hat, grow a beard, and be a farmer (or wear a head doily and dress modestly)."

My point is that the Amish are so out of touch with the reality of modern culture that their Christian witness is a private affair with no power to impact the world around them. That is how some churches and Christians will be if they continue to avoid social media and modern culture. Fortunately, the pandemic has awakened the church and believers to the power of social media, but time will tell if it is a permanent awakening or if we return to our old-fashioned ways when the all clear signal is given.

Let me say before we proceed that I am not insinuating social media will replace the Church. Face-to-face contact is always the norm for worship and Christian assembly. I am saying, however, that there is much more the church can do to incorporate technology into its ministry work, not as an afterthought but as an important part. And in a time of crisis like we are currently experiencing, social media is the next best thing to being present with one another.

TECHNOLOGY

Since I continually use the word *technology*, it would be good to define the term before we proceed. I don't want to get too technical (pardon the pun) so let's go with one definition I found on the Internet (a great example of the use of technology):

> *Science or knowledge put into practical use to solve problems or invent useful tools* (found in yourdictionary. com).

Another definition is

> *Technology is a body of knowledge devoted to creating tools, processing actions, and the extracting of materials. The term 'technology' is wide, and everyone has their way of understanding its meaning. We use technology to accomplish various tasks in our daily lives, in brief; we can describe technology as products and processes used to simplify our daily lives. We use technology to extend our abilities, making people the most crucial part of any technological system* (from www.whatistechnology.com).

I have found that we tend to label something technology if it is new in our lifetime, while taking older technology for granted. For example, we would probably not consider a refrigerator as technology, unless it has some of the newer features now available, like an ice maker or an automatic temperature control that prevents opening the freezer if the temperature in the freezer is above a certain level. Yet at one time, that refrigerator represented a technological advance over an icebox.

Therefore, someone born before social media sees it as technology but someone who was born after social media may not see it as technology, just a means of communication.

This is important because we must look back on the ministry of Paul to see that he used the technology of his day to spread his gospel. He did not categorize what he used as technology because he was accustomed to its existence.

For example, Paul wrote letters to the churches he founded. That is an example of technology. He used pen, ink, and paper or papyrus scrolls. Then he sent those letters with carriers who traveled on Roman roads or through Roman sea lanes, both of which were technological advances. When Paul wrote to a region, he ordered his letters to be read in all the area churches, so in a sense, he ordered his messages to go viral.

Today, we read Paul's letters because of technology. Fourteen hundred years after Paul wrote, a man named Gutenberg invented the printing press and suddenly books could be copied not by hand but by a machine someone operated. Eventually, people could own their own Bibles whereas before they could only access a copy that had been transcribed by hand (the same way Paul had written—with pen, ink, and paper).

As explorers set out to discover the world, the technological tools of travel improved and that eventually connected people all over the world. That connection continued as new forms of technology emerged, things like the telegraph, the telephone, radio, television, cassettes, iPods, CDs, DVDs, smart phones, and now the Internet. Excuse this quite cursory, simplistic overview of 2,000 years of technological history, but the points I am trying to make are these:

1. The technological advances have been God's will, for they have contributed to His desire that people exercise dominion over the earth.

2. The Church has always used the technology of the day for its own purposes of disseminating the gospel and training the followers of Jesus.

Now, you may not like how some radio or television preachers or evangelists have used the technology, but you cannot deny technology has been utilized in many other situations for good. The same is true for the Internet; there is tremendous evil and misinformation in cyberspace, but there is a wealth of valuable information that has been and can be used for good as well.

This phenomenon has led to this generation being the best-informed group of people in the history of the world, and perhaps the least socialized—at least in the Western world. People are glued to their smart phones and some young people would rather text than talk. Also, the shallow, frivolous use of social media has alienated some and prevented them from seeing how social media can be used beyond informing friends and followers that "I am in the mall" or "just got my haircut" or "where can I buy the cheapest tires for my car?"

Enough of the philosophical aspects of a theology. Is there a biblical basis or mandate to use technology for ministry purposes, perhaps even for church meetings? Let's take a look in the next chapter.

CHAPTER 15
QUESTIONS FOR DISCUSSION OR STUDY

1. What impressed you most from this chapter's material?

2. What changes will what you learned make in your approach to technology?

3. How would you evaluate your personal use of social media based on the material in this chapter?

4. How would you evaluate your church's use of social media based on the material in this chapter?

5. Am I overstating the problem or its consequences with the spiritual Amish analogy? Why or why not?

A THEOLOGY OF WRITING, BROADCASTING, AND SOCIAL MEDIA

Let's look at the definition of technology I included in the previous chapter:

> *Technology is a body of knowledge devoted to creating tools, processing actions, and the extracting of materials. The term 'technology' is wide, and everyone has their way of understanding its meaning. We use technology to accomplish various tasks in our daily lives, in brief; we can describe technology as products and processes used to simplify our daily lives. We use technology to extend our abilities, making people the most crucial part of any technological system* (from www.whatistechnology.com).

Is there a theology of technology, if I can label it that,

that extends even to the use of social media? I believe there is, so let me present my case. You be the judge if it's valid.

As we start, I confess that this overview represents an overkill of sorts. If you are interested in further study or if you still need convinced the technology and social media "thing" are from God, I would encourage you to read through this chapter and consider the validity of the case I make. If you are already convinced, feel free to move on to the next chapter. Lets get started.

1. "Now write down this song and teach it to the Israelites and have them sing it, so that it may be a witness for me against them" – Deuteronomy 31:19.

God had Israel compose a song to remember, but in this case, the theme was to commemorate their unfaithfulness. We compose and write to help people remember God's faithfulness, even when we are unfaithful to Him and His ways.

2. "Appoint three men from each tribe. I will send them out to make a survey of the land and to write a description of it, according to the inheritance of each. Then they will return to me" – Joshua 18:4.

God asked the scouts to submit a report of what they saw. I am not sure why He required it in writing, but perhaps it was so they could keep the vision alive of what God had promised them. The same holds true for us. We write and broadcast what we see in faith, which may be something that cannot be yet seen except through the eyes of faith. Then once it happens, we can look back and see how God led us along the way and was faithful to His word and promises.

3. As the men started on their way to map out the land, Joshua instructed them, "Go and make a survey of the land and write a description of it." – Joshua 18:8

It is interesting that the people could write at this early

stage of history. This would have represented an early form of technology using papyrus and ink to record words that could be read and understood by others.

> 4. "Go now, write it on a tablet for them, inscribe it on a scroll, that for the days to come it may be an everlasting witness." – Isaiah 30:8

We are not writing anything that compares to the inspired word of God, yet we should write down or send out what we believe God is showing us—about His word, His promises, our experiences, our creative interpretations of truth capable of communicating that truth and God's beauty to others—all with a view toward providing a witness for future generations concerning God's love and acts. Think of those who did this: John Wesley, St. Augustine, St. Thomas a Kempis, John Calvin, D. L. Moody, G. Campbell Morgan, and Martin Luther, just to name a few. Aren't you glad they didn't simply rely on the spoken word but made the effort and invested the time to record what they heard and saw for us to consider today?

> 5. "This is what the Lord, the God of Israel, says: 'Write in a book all the words I have spoken to you." – Jeremiah 30:2
>
> "Take a scroll and write on it all the words I have spoken to you concerning Israel, Judah and all the other nations from the time I began speaking to you in the reign of Josiah till now." – Jeremiah 36:2
>
> "Take another scroll and write on it all the words that were on the first scroll, which Jehoiakim king of Judah burned up." – Jeremiah 36:28

The prophets of old were not only to speak the word of the Lord, they were also to write it down. The very fact the Lord commanded His people to write indicates He expected them to use technology of some sort, for writing must be produced, published, and disseminated for it to be meaningful and have an effect.

6. "With this in mind, since I myself have carefully investigated everything from the beginning, I too decided to write an orderly account for you, most excellent Theophilus" – Luke 1:3.

Notice Luke did not claim that the Lord directed him to write; it was a natural decision based on the request from Theophilus for more information about the life and times of Jesus. Then Luke the doctor scientist utilized his excellent Greek and interviewing and fact-gathering skills to write two books about Jesus and His legacy in the early Church.

7. "Further, my brothers and sisters, rejoice in the Lord! It is no trouble for me to write the same things to you again, and it is a safeguard for you." – Philippians 3:1

Don't wait until you have a thought or idea that no one else in the universe has ever had. Don't be concerned that you are writing something already said or written by someone else. There is nothing new under the sun, but your perspective, vocabulary, background, or insight can make the difference in someone understanding something they have seen before—for some reason, they heard something from you enabling God to open their heart to receive it. It is also good for people to be reminded of the truth they once knew but perhaps have lost in the quagmire of daily life and mental clutter.

8. "I do not write to you because you do not know the truth, but because you do know it and because no lie comes from the truth" – 1 John 2:21.

Some people think, "Why should I write a book about this or that? There are already so many books on that topic." And that is why you write—to add your perspective or your two cents to what is a common topic of interest. Consider this example. People who are counselors are usually looking for new insight in their field. To contribute something to that discipline is important, even though there are already many books on that general topic. The same would be true of theology, testimonies, Bible studies, and works of fiction.

> 9. "We proclaim to you what we have seen and heard, so that you also may have fellowship with us. And our fellowship is with the Father and with his Son, Jesus Christ. We write this to make our joy complete." – 1 John 1:3-4

John wrote so they could have fellowship with one another and with God. One of the common complaints about social media and technology is that they are impersonal and don't build relationships. John implied, however, that his technology of sending a letter did indeed contribute to the values and practice of fellowship and relationships. John also stated writing made his joy complete, indicating there was something missing in his spiritual makeup if he did not write to people with whom he had a close relationship when he was not physically near to them.

> 10. What then shall we say, brothers and sisters? When you come together, each of you has a hymn, or a word of instruction, a revelation, a tongue or an interpretation. Everything must be done so that the church may be built up. – 1 Corinthians 14:26
>
> ...speaking to one another with psalms, hymns, and songs from the Spirit. Sing and make music from your heart to the Lord. – Ephesians 5:19

Social media and broadcasting, done properly, take you out of yourself and into the lives and worlds of other people. When you go there, you should bring something of value with you. That is the reason why I don't use my social media outlets or technology for trivial matters. Yes, I do post my destinations when I am traveling, and I also post pictures of sporting events I attend. I do that for a reason, however, which is to demonstrate to my followers that I am doing what I love (travel and sports). I am directly or indirectly encouraging them to do something in their own lives that stimulates and energizes them.

I take every encounter I have with every person seriously, and I attempt to apply the commands found in Corinthians and Ephesians to bring a revelation or a message that will uplift, inspire, or entertain.

11. "What I tell you in the dark, speak in the daylight; what is whispered in your ear, proclaim from the roofs." – Matthew 10:27

If I have something the Lord has showed me, then I am obligated to share it with others who may find it helpful as well. I am also informed in Revelation 12:11 that "they triumphed over him by the blood of the Lamb and by the word of their testimony; they did not love their lives so much as to shrink from death." When is the last time you gave a testimony in a church setting about something God did in your life? Probably not any time in recent memory, but social media gives you the perfect means to do so!

12. After this letter has been read to you, see that it is also read in the church of the Laodiceans and that you in turn read the letter from Laodicea. – Colossians 4:16

Paul wanted everyone in the area of Colossae to hear his letter and then they were to hear the one he sent to Laodicea as well. This tells us that Paul wrote more letters than we have today. What's more, Paul ordered his letters to go "viral," wanting everyone in both areas to read and hear both letters. Paul used technology to stay in touch with, educate, and disciple his flock, and he expected them to put in the time and effort to read what he wrote.

13. Dear friends, this is now my second letter to you. I have written both of them as reminders to stimulate you to wholesome thinking. – 2 Peter 3:1

Using technology requires that we "get over ourselves" and our fear of criticism or what others will think of us. That is because we have been taught not to draw attention to ourselves, so when we do that through some creative expression, we can be tormented with guilt or be the targets of criticism. Peter wrote a letter that did not contain any new material, but he wrote to ensure his readers were engaged in what he termed wholesome thinking. He wrote not to satisfy his needs but to meet the needs of others. He was not concerned that someone would see his work as redundant or simple. He wrote because he wanted to write. We should do the same.

> 14. And what more shall I say? I do not have time to tell about Gideon, Barak, Samson and Jephthah, about David and Samuel and the prophets . . ."
> - Hebrews 11:32.

I find it unusual that a man writing a letter would write "I don't have time" or "what more shall I say?" There is a theory that the letter to the Hebrews was not a letter at all, but rather a transcribed sermon. This coincides with a verse from Psalm 45:1 that says, "My heart is stirred by a noble theme as I recite my verses for the king; my tongue is the pen of a skillful writer." The psalmist was composing verses, reading them to the king, and then those words were written down. Do you see how technology (the written aspect) emanated from the spoken word? That tells me you don't have to write but when you speak, rhyme, paint, sculp, dance, sing, or express any other form of creativity, you should look for as many ways as possible to share what you have done—and that is where technology can become your friend.

> 15. Let the redeemed of the Lord tell their story—those he redeemed from the hand of their foe.
> – Psalm 107:2

One generation commends your works to another;

they tell of your mighty acts. They speak of the glorious splendor of your majesty—and I will meditate on your wonderful works. They tell of the power of your awesome works—and I will proclaim your great deeds. They celebrate your abundant goodness and joyfully sing of your righteousness. – Psalm 145:4-7

They triumphed over him by the blood of the Lamb and by the word of their testimony; they did not love their lives so much as to shrink from death. – Revelation 12:11

We are not urged to share our testimony. It is not a suggestion or a good idea, something we get around to when we have the time. No, we are *commanded* to share our stories and testimonies of God's faithfulness. It is to keep a record for the next generation so they won't forget and will add their stories to the family record as well. What's more, our testimonies have spiritual power for they enable and empower us to overcome the adversary of our soul.

When is the last time you shared a testimony in a live church service? It is probably not any time lately if ever. Technology provides the perfect vehicle to share your insights and stories of God's faithfulness to you and yours. Then you will have the confident to take on bigger, more complex projects like books, plays, businesses, paintings, and major arts and crafts (like furnishings or building projects).

16. Then Jesus came to them and said, "All authority in heaven and on earth has been given to me. Therefore go and make disciples of all nations, baptizing them in the name of the Father and of the Son and of the Holy Spirit, and teaching them to obey everything I have commanded you. And surely I am with you always, to the very end of the age" – Matthew 28:18-20

Those words of Jesus have come to be known as the Great Commission. We are to go to the ends of the earth to preach, teach, and disciple—and He promises to go with us. Technology enables us all to fulfill that Commission whether we can afford or like to travel or not. The problem is, however, that most of us don't feel ready or equipped to go beyond the door of our church. We are so paralyzed by fear of doing the wrong thing, getting ahead of the Lord, or any number of other restrictive thoughts that we can't begin to think of how or what we would use the technology to say or do beyond our family, friends, or members.

That is where the Church should come in to equip and empower all its members, not just leadership, to use technology not as an end, but as a means to an end—which is to express their purpose and showcase their creativity. What's more, churches should lead the way by modeling creative, consistent, and valuable expressions of God's love and work through social media channels.

There you have a basic theology or Bible study on the use of technology. You may be thinking, "That all seemed to be directed more toward the individual and not the Church as a whole." That is true. We must accept the fact that each of us as individuals must have a philosophy for our use and application of technology and cannot delegate that job to the Church. Once we have that in place for ourselves, then it will be a natural progression that we will help and expect our church to have done the same thing. If a church is made up of members who are indifferent or hostile to technology, then that church will have the same mindset.

Having said that, let's move on to the next chapter where I will present a simple solution to the challenge of technology for the modern church and that is the position I refer to as an Online Pastor. Let's go there now.

CHAPTER 16
QUESTIONS FOR DISCUSSION OR STUDY

1. What impressed you most from this chapter's material?

2. What changes will what you learned make in your approach to technology?

3. How would you evaluate your personal use of social media based on the material in this chapter?

4. How would you evaluate your church's use of social media based on the material in this chapter?

5. Are there any others examples from the Bible that could be added to our theology of social media and technology?

A SIMPLE SOLUTION
FOR EVERY CHURCH

In the previous section, I recommended that each church appoint a purpose pastor, someone who can help people recognize and then engage their purpose through appropriate actions like publishing, starting a business, being more creative, or entering into full-time church work. To go along with the purpose pastor, I also recommend that every church identify and release a pastor of social media and technology. Notice I used the word *release* for this person will need to be freed from preconceived notions of how technology should be utilized in order to pave new roads for church ministry.

I will not get too specific as to this person's job description, but in general, it will be to

> take who we are as a people—what we teach, how we worship, what we believe, how we apply what we believe, our church ministries—and make that accessible not only to those in closest proximity to our church but in way that reaches to "the ends of the earth."

This position will not allow a church's presence online to be an afterthought or something that is done when the church gets around to it. The online pastor will make social media and technology a top priority. They will have the full cooperation of all the staff and in a sense will co-pastor the church with the lead pastor, mutually submitting to one another. Due to the priority that lead pastors tend to give to the face-to-face church presence, this online pastor and his or her team must have unprecedented authority to make decisions in the best interests of the online work, sometimes at the expense of the live worship experience. This online pastor will have permission to involve any and all church staff and members in this endeavor.

For example, let's say that the senior pastor shares a message that is well received by the people. The online pastor can decide to turn that series into a book, an online series with a study guide, or put it in any other format necessary to fulfill his or her mandate and *the senior pastor cannot refuse.* The online pastor can assign any staff member online duties and they cannot refuse or claim it's not their strength or gift, or resort to the "I am too busy" excuse. To give another example, the online pastor can decide the church is going to live broadcast the youth or children's ministry and that's that. There can be no protests from either department that they don't want to do this.

If you are experienced in church work, you may protest as you think of all the reasons this cannot or should not happen. Let me give you another example of how it could and why it should. A church I have worked with had a midweek club for children that ran on Wednesday and Thursday nights. When attendance dwindled, they eliminated the Wednesday night and kept the Thursday events going. There is nothing wrong with that. An online pastor, however, would never have agreed to that decision without investigating how that midweek club could be replaced with an online version.

Therefore, the online pastor would reason, "The children are staying at home so let's reach them there. We are going to develop online activities to replace the Wednesday night event so the children and their parents can utilize and benefit from those activities any night of the week convenient for them." Again, if you are experienced, you will think, *The church doesn't have the staff to do that.* It's true, the church doesn't because the church has never made it a priority. The online pastor will need to build a team from among the available membership to assist in this endeavor, especially younger people themselves who can help do the work.

I know I am being simplistic in my answers here because the objections you may raise are legitimate and not easily overcome—but they are not insurmountable. My assumption is that all the resources any church needs to fulfill its mission are sitting in their midst. The church needs new eyes to see who is present and utilize those people in a more effective way. This is also where the purpose pastor can help the online pastor, for the purpose pastor will be close to who knows and does what in the church, and also to whom God is speaking about more involvement in the church's ministry work.

MORE POSSIBILITIES

Another aspect of the duties for the technology pastor will be to identify and build a team that will provide an online presence during the live worship services. The members of that team will use their own social media presence, or the church's, to publish and broadcast portions of the live service. That will include quotes from the sermon, perhaps a line from a song sung that impressed them, or their own insight as the service progresses: "Pastor Sam is preaching from 1 Samuel 1. I have never thought of Hannah as he is presenting her. Good stuff!"

Furthermore, the technology pastor will then help each

staff member with their own social media philosophy, helping them spell out exactly how and when they personally will engage social media, which media they will use, and what they will include in their online presence. This may be a weekly blog, a regular video update, a devotional, or a podcast. Where the technical savvy is lacking, the pastor will provide training.

Then the technology pastor will do the same for any in the church who are interested in doing the same. He or she will start by imparting a theology of social media, reinforced from the pulpit, to help people overcome any latent bias against the new technology. Then the online pastor will help people understand how to use technology in a way consistent with their personal ministry or purpose.

In 2014, I started my publishing company, Urban Press. Because the members knew me, I have now completed book projects for many people in my church. What's my point? The online pastor in a church would be the one to help the membership with their publishing goals, including poetry, kids' books, and testimonies.

The online pastor, in partnership with the purpose pastor, will sponsor teaching seminars on creativity, with the main focus on helping people overcome their fear to create and publish online. I have observed how fearful people in church are lest they promote themselves (more on that in the Appendix) or draw attention to their own person instead of the Lord. This is why there needs to be a concerted effort to help both staff and membership overcome the fear that began when Adam and Eve hid from God in the bushes because they were ashamed and afraid (see Genesis 3).

Other possible ways to promote and highlight creativity and purpose while also using technology in the ministry of the church could include:

- Art exhibits
- Book signings

- Using social media to indicate presence at church services

- Having those present submit questions on the sermon during the service and allowing time to answer those questions as part of the preached message. Any unanswered questions can be handled after the service is over through, you guessed it, social media.

- Encouraging a team of people present during the services to post quotes from and impressions of the service on their own social media. A designated team can do the same on the church's media.

- Providing training for older saints or those who do not have access to technology or the knowledge of how to use what they have. This may include providing computers or smartphones for those who can't afford them.

- Reinforcement from senior leadership that technology is a vital part of the congregation's mission.

MORE OBSTACLES

I have often quoted 2 Timothy 1:7 to people who were facing fear where their purpose and creativity were concerned: "For the Spirit God gave us does not make us timid, but gives us power, love and self-discipline." Until recently, I had never quoted verse six, which provides the context for the fear: "For this reason I remind you to fan into flame the gift of God, which is in you through the laying on of my hands." What is the context for the fear? It is the person's gift. They are to fan that gift into flame, but they will usually be hesitant to do that. Both the online and the purpose pastor can help people recognize fear for what it is and where it is restricting appropriate action, and then help them take steps to move on.

Some congregations have already experimented with an online church service with its own team that oversees the broadcast. This includes a prayer team ready to field prayer requests, greeters who respond to comments or questions during the service, ushers to "receive" the offering, and evangelists to monitor the altar call who are ready to pray and follow up with those who respond. During the pandemic, churches have been forced to do more online and in a manner that is more engaging and personalized. I can only hope this continues when the pandemic has run its course.

I can hear even more objections being raised as I write these possibilities for greater, more purposeful use of technology in the life of the church.

- "We are too busy for this." That is the reason you must have a separate team that has no face-to-face duties in charge of these initiatives.

- "This isn't church." I agree, but what we learned during the pandemic is that going to church online was the next best thing to being there. Churches had "visitors" from all over the world, finances in many cases remained stable (if churches had the means for people to give online), expenses went down (no building maintenance or utility usage), and people's spiritual needs were met through prayer and counseling (how would we have made it without Zoom or Teams?).

- "What about relationships?" My church had all their small group meetings during the pandemic using Zoom and attendance went up. People stayed in touch and needs were met. Yes, they had relationships with one another before the pandemic, and technology can never take the

place of a hug or a handshake (scratch the handshake in the post-pandemic world), but we have
consistently underestimated the power of technology to enhance and even start relationships
(25% of all couples today meet online).

Now let me raise some further reasons to do what I
have recommended in this chapter if you decide not to make a
full commitment to a vibrant online presence using the technology available to you.

- We read in Acts 20:35 that it is better to give
then receive. If you have a chance to "give' away
who you are as a people or to share what God
is doing for you as an individual or church, it is
the equivalent of lighting a candle. If you don't
share it by every means available, it is like placing
it under a bushel.

- There is only so much you can do during the
few hours the church assembles to disciple, train,
and engage people where they are at. Technology
gives them access to resources for growth and
development 24/7.

- When you don't give the world access to who
you are, what you know, and what God has given
you to do, you delegate the Great Commission
to a chosen few. You abdicate personal responsibility to do what you can to spread the good
news.

- If you have something that could benefit people in other churches, you have an obligation to
make it available if they choose to pay attention
or access it. Read what Paul wrote concerning
the Thessalonians:

And so you became a model to all the believers in

Macedonia and Achaia. The Lord's message rang out from you not only in Macedonia and Achaia—your faith in God has become known everywhere. Therefore we do not need to say anything about it, for they themselves report what kind of reception you gave us. They tell how you turned to God from idols to serve the living and true God, and to wait for his Son from heaven, whom he raised from the dead—Jesus, who rescues us from the coming wrath (1 Thessalonians 1:7-10).

Paul commended them for the good testimony that was having an impact on other believers throughout the region.

When the pandemic hit, here was my response to the situation.

- Facebook Live thirty-minute sessions three times a week.

- An hour-long blog radio show Monday through Friday.

- I edited a daily devotional from one of my five published devotional books Monday through Friday, and then posted it to Facebook, LinkedIn, Twitter, and my ministry mobile app, which I launched one month into the pandemic

- Multiple daily short, inspirational posts on all social media, but especially my Facebook personal page. I am now in the process of publishing these under the title *Pandemic Proverbs: Wisdom from the Lockdown*.

- Reactivated my Facebook pages for Urban Press and PurposeQuest International.

- I wrote a weekly post in my *Live the Word* Bible study focusing on creativity and purpose in the book of Genesis. I posted it to my blog, on Facebook, Twitter, and LinkedIn. You guessed it; it will become a book when it is finished.

- I published a weekly post on my personal blog that focused on leadership or other general interest issues.

- I continued my weekly entry on my *Monday Memo* site, which has 965 entries as of this writing.

- I maintained regular communication with those who write or post comments. I also had a rotating schedule to call those who were on my heart to stay in touch during the crisis.

- I began a six-week online study course on the topic of creativity. I had sponsored face-to-face meetings at my church and the attendance had dwindled to five or six people. The online course had 20 people enrolled. This is a typical report during the pandemic as churches saw increased "attendance" for their programs when they put them online.

If this is what one man can do and do it effectively, what could a team of dedicated church members and volunteers produce that reflects and expresses the life of Christ through the Spirit in their midst?

This new section is not meant to provide a checklist of things for you to do to have a more profound online presence. It is intended to get you thinking and to give you examples of some of the possibilities available to you and the reasons why you should consider doing them.

One of the most significant objections I hear to the use of social media is that it is narcissistic and self-promoting, glorifying self (through selfies and other expressions of self) with trivial self-centered material. There is no question this is how some people utilize their social media, which is an underutilization of a valuable resource. Yet because some misuse their computer to watch bad things does that mean we should not use our computers for good?

If you are interested in my response to this objection, I will not include it here, for I fear I have made this chapter long enough. Instead, I will wrap up this section, and make further arguments for social media in the Appendix. There I will address the topics of self-promotion and drawing attention to one's self to see if we can better understand how to avoid those pitfalls in the use of God-given technology. Much of what is in the Appendix was written on my *Monday Memo* site well before the pandemic, so they are in the format I use for that weekly program.

CHAPTER 17
QUESTIONS FOR DISCUSSION OR STUDY

1. What impressed you most from this chapter's material?
2. What changes will what you learned make in your approach to technology?
3. How would you evaluate your personal use of social media based on the material in this chapter?
4. How would you evaluate your church's use of social media based on the material in this chapter?
5. What new ideas or strategies occurred to you while you read this chapter? What is your plan to implement them?
6. What are the obstacles in your life, or the life of your church, preventing further or more effective use of social media?

★★★★★

Before we move on to the Epilogue, let's take a look at the Eight Steps, together for the first time at the end of this new section:

1. Raise up an army of purpose-led men and women who have faith to do the impossible, freed from trying to be who they are not and released to be the fullest, best expression of who God created them to be.

2. Equip people to perform missions (both domestic and foreign), to launch business ventures, and to carry out any other activity their purpose dictates and faith allows.

3. Help leaders be productive in their purpose as they oversee Holy Spirit chaos created by people pursuing and fulfilling their purpose.

4. Help leaders and governing bodies move from attitudes of ownership to attitudes of servant-leadership and stewardship.

5. Develop services, Sunday Schools, kid's church, youth meetings, and even committee meetings that people want to attend because they involve a spirit of excellence and the unexpected.

6. Move from fads, copycat programs, and trite and phony rituals, traditions, and doctrines to innovative initiatives in the Spirit of (but exceeding the results of) the early church.

7. Address and meet the needs of the poor, ethnic minorities, and women around the world.

8. Utilize technology and social media not as an afterthought or sideshow but as something equal in importance to face-to-face ministry.

EPILOGUE

When I was doing the final edits on this section, I wrote two blog entries about creativity and innovation in churches. I thought they would be the perfect end to this section and to this revised book before we move on to the Appendix. They speak for themselves and tie in nicely with what we have discussed. I will make some comments at the end.

★★★★★

INNOVATIVE OR CREATIVE?

There are many byproducts and interesting trends emerging from the pandemic of 2020. One is the struggle for economies to re-open. Part of the problem is that we have learned to live with so much less that many are hesitant to spend cash on what they can live without. It has also caused us to step back and see where our economy has gone over the last decade. In my estimation, much of our creativity has gone into making what already exists a little better or a little different. For example, the first microbrewery was innovative, but do we need hundreds of them? Probably not. The same is true for yoghurt shops, health spas, and retail stores selling cheap junk from China.

My main focus, however, has not been the economy but the Church during this season. As I write, some churches are reopening, having done a "deep cleaning" with seats spaced for appropriate social distancing. During the pandemic, I saw a lot of creativity from the church, but I did not see a lot of innovation—the creative use of something that changes culture and not just an expression of existing cultural values or norms.

Let me give you an example of what I consider innovation and you will understand what I mean.

THE SYNAGOGUE

Did you ever give any thought to where the synagogue came from or how or why it emerged? There is no mention of a synagogue in the Old Testament. The first mention is in the gospels and by then, it was an important part of Jewish life and worship. How did it become so popular and prominent?

It seems the Jews had a pandemic of their own in 586 BC when Nebuchadnezzar ransacked Jerusalem and the Temple with it. The entire focus of Jewish life had revolved around the Temple and the sacrificial system, but then suddenly, just like we experienced in the pandemic, their worship focus was gone.

Some of the Jews stayed behind in Jerusalem but most who survived were carried off to Babylon, home to many temples devoted to idols that were off limits to Jews. What did the Jews do? They innovated. They adjusted from the Temple system with animal sacrifice to the synagogue where reading and study of the Word were the main emphases. When they returned to Judea 70 years later, they did eventually rebuild the Temple, but by then the synagogue was firmly established as an important part of their worship culture.

THE IMPLICATIONS

Where am I going with all this? Churches rushed to use social media during the pandemic, some that had been vocal opponents of its use prior to the pandemic. They had the attitude "social media and technology are an abomination to the Lord . . . and an ever-present help in time of trouble." Many saw their "numbers" go up and their finances hold steady (those who still refused to engage it cannot wait to reopen for their lifeline to the people had been cut off). Some gave testimony that people were "watching" them from foreign countries and some saw people surrender their lives to the Lord through the use of technology.

We saw churches do drive-in churches using their car radios. We had drive through prayer and healing lines. There were many other examples of creativity, but now that the "pressure" is relieved, can we still be creative? We were also creative in our deployment of technology, but can we now also be innovative?

- Can we take questions during our live services using Facebook or Twitter and use the last 10 minutes of our message time to answer some of those questions to ensure the people "got" what we were preaching? Can we then answer the other questions after the service throughout the week using social media?

- Can we designate an online church team to monitor who is watching or listening via social media, to pray with any who have needs, or to "welcome" them as we would during a live service?

- Can we *not* finish a Sunday message and direct people to "tune in" on Sunday evening to hear the conclusion?

- How about we develop online devotions for parents to use with their children during the summer and even throughout the school year?

- Would it be possible to continue our online Zoom Bible studies and small groups?

- Are there other social media initiatives we can continue after the all-clear is given to meet?

These are only a few of the ideas I can come up with that I consider both creative *and* innovative to help us make the transition from Jerusalem to Babylon as the Jews had to do. I would suggest social media could be our synagogue-like response to current events. As we rush back to church, and well we should if we can and it is safe, let us not forget the lesson of the pandemic that technology is the next best thing to being there. It has shown us the possibilities for a whole new concept of the church's mission.

★★★★★

THE WISE WAY

In the previous essay, I discussed innovation and creativity, pointing out that the pandemic caused churches to be creative in their use of technology. I used the example of the synagogue as an example of an innovation that was creatively deployed in Jewish history, and was wondering what innovations will emerge from this season—or if in our rush to reopen our churches, we will abandon ongoing creative use of technology that could lead to something fresh and new in the way churches deliver their "services."

If you have ever heard one of my purpose presentations, you heard me start at Acts 6:1-7 where the apostles chose men to carry out the burden of the work among the widows (and you have seen this passage referred to throughout this book):

> In those days when the number of disciples was increasing, the Hellenistic Jews among them complained against the Hebraic Jews because their widows were being overlooked in the daily distribution of food. So the Twelve gathered all the disciples together and said, "It would not be right for us to neglect the ministry of the word of God in order to wait on tables. Brothers and sisters, choose seven men from among you who are known to be full of the Spirit and wisdom. We will turn this responsibility over to them and will give our attention to

prayer and the ministry of the word." This proposal pleased the whole group. They chose Stephen, a man full of faith and of the Holy Spirit; also Philip, Procorus, Nicanor, Timon, Parmenas, and Nicolas from Antioch, a convert to Judaism. They presented these men to the apostles, who prayed and laid their hands on them. So the word of God spread. The number of disciples in Jerusalem increased rapidly, and a large number of priests became obedient to the faith.

The people elected those men to serve or minister to the widows in the church, and the Greek word for service here is *diakonia*, from which we derive our modern church office of or word *deacon*.

Many churches have taken this passage in Acts 6 and turned it into a model for church government and service. In some churches, the deacons are the ultimate governing authority; in others, they are people who serve by doing practical things in the church like building care, women's ministry, and the like. The goal of this essay is not to debate which approach to or interpretation of deacons is correct; the goal is to show that any approach to deacons as a church institution misses the point altogether. The original deacons were not about church government or tradition; they were simply an innovative solution to a new problem.

THE BACKGROUND

As best we can tell, there was no biblical precedent upon which the apostles drew to elect and commission the deacons. Jesus had instructed them to care for the poor and most widows were poor in the early church if they had no other family to care for them. As the church grew, the number of widows increased to include those outside the ranks of the Hebrew residents in Jerusalem. The apostles were being called upon to address this problem they had never before faced. It is interesting Luke was careful to point out the problem was between two ethnic groups, the Hebraic and the Hellenistic believers, which shows us ethnic tensions existed even in the early church.

The apostles addressed this problem creatively, using wisdom to come up with an innovative solution. I don't believe they were instituting a church office in Acts 6 as stated previously, but rather modeling an approach the Church should take to solve problems and challenges that are sure to come up in every generation—whether in or outside the church. They were setting a precedent, not establishing a tradition.

THE IMPLICATIONS

When I reflect on creativity and innovation, I think of the verses in Proverbs 8:22-31 where we learn wisdom was at God's side when He created the universe:

"The Lord brought me forth as the first of his works, before his deeds of old; I was formed long ages ago, at the very beginning, when the world came to be. When there were no watery depths, I was given birth, when there were no springs overflowing with water; before the mountains were settled in place, before the hills, I was given birth, before he made the world or its fields or any of the dust of the earth. I was there when he set the heavens in place, when he marked out the horizon on the face of the deep, when he established the clouds above and fixed securely the fountains of the deep, when he gave the sea its boundary so the waters would not overstep his command, and when he marked out the foundations of the earth. Then I was constantly at his side. I was filled with delight day after day, rejoicing always in his presence, rejoicing in his whole world and delighting in mankind."

Wisdom is closely related to creativity, which leads to my definition of creativity:

> *the wise application of knowledge to existing problems or opportunities in such a way that something new and innovative emerges.*

In Acts 6, the problem was the care for widows. The biblical precedent that existed was the instance when Moses selected helpers (or something akin to deacons) because he was overwhelmed; later, elections were also common in Israel to elect synagogue leaders. Therefore, the apostles applied existing knowledge (getting leaders some help and holding elections for those helpers) in a new way—a *wise* way—to address a current problem and the result was creativity: a group of men who we label *deacons* today.

What's my point? The church should be the bastion and vanguard of creativity because we have the Creative Spirit of God in our midst. We should not look to solve new problems with the solutions of the past. We are unnecessarily bound to our traditions when we don't see creativity as a function of the Church and believers, or when fear causes us to retreat to the tried-and-true *procedures* rather than experiment with new *applications* of tried-and-true wisdom principles that lead to innovation.

I urge you not to settle for what's been done but take what's been done and pioneer something that has never been done. The world is not waiting for us to debate the role of deacons, but to find 21st century solutions to modern challenges that are the equal of what the apostles did in Acts 6. When we do, we will be working with the wisdom of Proverbs 8 that was present when God created and structured the world. One thing is certain: There is no greater creativity with which you and I can work than anything infused with the Spirit of God.

★★★★★

What we have discussed in this book, and especially in this new section on technology and social media, does indeed represent a reformation of the Church, perhaps as dramatic as the one that began when Martin Luther nailed his 95 Theses to the door of the Wittenberg Cathedral in 1517. It is a plan to make the church less top-heavy with tradition, outdated leadership styles, and old delivery systems for the spiritual services and resources the world and its members need.

As I have stated elsewhere, this is not really about technology, but about leadership. Will a new leadership emerge that sees the need for the Church to change or will leaders be content to serve out their terms tweaking rather than tearing down and rebuilding the Church's communication strategies—while also re-examining and redirecting its missional outreach? The Church represents the kingdom of God on Earth, and it exists both to equip the saints who are members and also to exalt the Lord for all the world to see. The gates of hell will continue to assail the Church, trying to muffle and confuse its message. Leaders must increasingly be clear that the Church does not exist to preserve tradition, but to challenge and redefine it with every generation.

My prayer is that the COVID-19 pandemic that has swept the globe will provide part of the incentive we need to change the way we do church. As I write, churches are emerging from total lockdown, trying to figure out how they will sanitize their facilities to meet health requirements and give people confidence to assemble without risk. My own sense is that the move to restart public meetings will dilute the need to continue the progress we saw in the utilization of technology during the stay-at-home order.

At the same time, I would expect attendance in public meetings to be reduced from pre-pandemic levels, which is bad news because attendance was already dwindling before the pandemic—and smaller numbers mean smaller offerings.

Maybe God will use less people which will lead to less money to provide the post-pandemic incentive to change. I hope so.

As we close, I think of Isaiah 52:7 that states, "How beautiful on the mountains are the feet of those who bring good news, who proclaim peace, who bring good tidings, who proclaim salvation, who say to Zion, 'Your God reigns!'" Paul referred to this verse when he wrote in Romans 10:14-15,

> How, then, can they call on the one they have not believed in? And how can they believe in the one of whom they have not heard? And how can they hear without someone preaching to them? And how can anyone preach unless they are sent? As it is written: "How beautiful are the feet of those who bring good news!"

Lord, help us preach the good news through every means and medium possible, and may we keep in mind the last words You spoke to Your disciples that became their marching orders as Your soldiers:

> "All authority in heaven and on earth has been given to me. Therefore go and make disciples of all nations, baptizing them in the name of the Father and of the Son and of the Holy Spirit, and teaching them to obey everything I have commanded you. And surely I am with you always, to the very end of the age" (Matthew 28:18-20).

Be with us as we seek to make the Church all it can be, all You want it to be, in this generation and in others to come until Your return. Amen.

APPENDICES
ONE
THROUGH
SEVEN

APPENDIX ONE

THE AUTHORITY
OF PURPOSE

I composed this email as part of a six-month weekly series titled "Put Me In, Coach." The premise was we can and must live a more assertive, bold lifestyle that seizes as many opportunities as possible to broadcast God's goodness and the work of the Spirit in the Church and in our lives. By now, of course you realize this can be most effectively done through the appropriate use of technology as expressed through social media. Also, since I am recommending every church have a purpose pastor, this will reinforce the importance of purpose in the growth of any church.

★★★★★

INVITE YOURSELF TO THE PARTY: THE AUTHORITY OF PURPOSE

I was getting ready to teach a class not too long ago when one of the students brought in a cake and snacks because it was her birthday. When I said, "You invited yourself to the party," it reminded me on a *Monday Memo* I wrote years ago titled, "Invite Yourself to the Party." I knew right away it fit in with our current theme, which is "Put Me In, Coach: Living a Bold Life." Let me explain with examples from my own life.

For years, I would be a guest on media shows, after which the host would rave about how well the show went—promising to have me back on the show soon. In almost every

172

instance, I was never invited back. Either they were lying that the show went well (I agreed with their assessment that it did go well), or they had no intention of asking me back (which meant they were lying), or they just did not follow through (they were sincere but inefficient).

Whatever the reason, I decided after so many disappointments to invite myself to the party: I sponsored my own weekly show on two AM stations for six years, as mentioned earlier, and I also hosted hundreds of blog radio shows. What's more, I started a Vimeo channel and have many video shows posted there and on Facebook. My point is that I was no longer content to be invited to the party. Just like my student, I threw my own party.

A CALL TO PURPOSE

I ran across this commentary I wrote eight years ago on Matthew 10:1-4. First, here is that passage, and then my comments:

> Jesus called his twelve disciples to him and gave them authority to drive out impure spirits and to heal every disease and sickness. These are the names of the twelve apostles: first, Simon (who is called Peter) and his brother Andrew; James son of Zebedee, and his brother John; Philip and Bartholomew; Thomas and Matthew the tax collector; James son of Alphaeus, and Thaddaeus; Simon the Zealot and Judas Iscariot, who betrayed him.

When God calls you to a purpose, He calls you by name and He calls you to Himself. It isn't just a task, it's a unique relationship with Him. I have found that when I function in my purpose, God provides for me and takes care of all I need to fulfill my purpose. He speaks to me, and my relationship with Him is somehow closer and more intimate when I am going about my purpose.

In Matthew, Jesus called twelve men to Himself and gave them authority. That was a question the Jews always asked Jesus: "By whose authority do You do these things?" Jesus did the things He did in the authority of His purpose. That is all the authority you need as well, for your purpose is your assignment from your heavenly headquarters. When you move in your purpose, you don't need an invitation to the party, so to speak. You invite yourself. Someone else described it as nominating yourself for the job.

AUTHORITY

If your purpose is to help the poor, you don't need anyone to invite you to do so. You show up where the poor are and help them. I was reflecting on this issue of authority recently and came up with nine aspects of purpose that give you the authority to do whatever it is God wants you to do—without an invitation. Here they are:

1. **The authority of results**: Your purpose helps you bear fruit. No one can question your authority when you can show them the fruit of your labors.

2. **The authority of clarity**: Your purpose is a clear, concise statement of what you are on earth to do. People will follow and respond to you because you are direct, clear, and focused.

3. **The authority of knowledge**: Your purpose enables and even drives you to be skilled at what you do. You will have more insight and knowledge about your sphere of purpose than others.

4. **The authority of calling**: God assigned your purpose and wants you to fulfill it even more than you do. He will open doors and create opportunities for you to succeed.

5. **The authority of integrity**: Your purpose

causes you to live by your values, those things that are most important to you. You don't want to undermine your purpose, so you have added incentive to be an honest person of your word.

6. **The authority of courage**: Your purpose makes you a leader where you function. You face your fears because your purpose is more important than you are. There are people waiting to benefit from what you do and who you are, so you press through obstacles to be there for them.

7. **The authority of success**: Your purpose gives you endurance to press through the barriers and endure long periods of suffering and frequent setbacks. You don't only achieve short-term results; you do so over a long period of time, which is defined as success

8. **The authority of humility**: You know your source of strength, which is God Himself. You acknowledge your source, but you don't deny you are good at what you do because you know God helps you produce results.

9. **The authority of honesty**: You do not engage in "false humility" (denying what you can do). You know and face your limitations and weaknesses with openness and transparency, and you do the same with your strengths.

When you have a purpose, you have all the authority you need to act. If you can't find a partner to help, you go it alone and wait for a partner to find you. If that doesn't happen, you are then content with the fact you have the most important partner of all, the Lord Himself, and together you will attend a purpose party impacting the lives of others and enriching your own.

If individuals have authority to act and speak, then how much more the Church of Jesus Christ, which is commissioned to spread the gospel and disciple believers. The Church does not need permission to do this for that has already been granted.

The beauty and challenge of social media is its unobtrusive ways. People choose to follow certain users of social media—or not. They may absorb most, some, a little, or none of what an individual or entity produces, even when they have chosen to grant that entity access to their attention and life.

APPENDIX TWO

PERMISSION MARKETING

*In this next three essays, I include the first series from my Monday Memo on a concept called **permission marketing**. I introduced this concept in Section Three when I discussed the influence that Seth Godin has had on my life and ministry. Don't be turned off by the secular nature of the concept, for it is upon this principle that I have established the work I do on and through technology. Read on and please be open to its relevance for our discussion that we must change the way we define and deliver church ministries and services.*

★★★★★

PERMISSION MARKETING 1

As you already know, I am a Seth Godin devotee. I think he is one of the best marketing thinkers today, but his work transcends marketing and speaks to leadership as well. His work influenced me to start *The Monday Memo* in 2001 and I believe his insight has great relevance for leaders, whether in business or church. Godin introduced me to the concept of *permission marketing*, which has implications for all of us who are leaders and is relevant to the topic of *Changing the Way We Do Church*.

Godin feels that most modern marketing doesn't work well because audiences being targeted didn't ask for it and don't want it. He points out that many marketers are looking to interrupt people with unwelcome ads, billboards, pop-up computer messages, and direct mail. Consequently, many people ignore or tune out those unwanted messages.

Godin argues that companies should invest money in creating remarkable products and services rather than spend the money for something like an ad for the Super Bowl broadcast that costs millions of dollars for a 30-second spot. Remarkable products are their own best marketing plan and word-of-mouth would spread the news like a virus, according to Godin. Thus, he also coined (or at least helped popularize) the term "idea virus." In light of the 2020 pandemic, we should all have an enhanced appreciation for what a virus can do and how quickly it can do it.

What makes more sense to Godin is *permission marketing* where people have asked for and welcome (or at least don't ignore) notices, ads, and material from a company (or church). My *Monday Memo* is an example of permission marketing. People have given me permission to send them what I write, and they are free to stop that connection at any time. They have given me their consent to share my thoughts, so therefore I am free to establish an online relationship with them. Here are some points to remember about permission marketing:

1. It costs time and money.
2. It is revocable and nontransferable; it can't be imposed on anyone else.
3. It doesn't happen by accident; it takes concerted effort and thought.
4. The relationships must be nurtured; there are no quick or easy results.
5. It is all about the recipient or the target audience and *not* about the company, service, product, church, or individual doing the marketing.

This is why most companies, nonprofits, churches, and organizations don't "get it" where permission marketing is concerned. It is too slow, too unspectacular, and too limited or restrictive. The old way of marketing needed mass markets, where permission marketing focuses on building relationships within a smaller niche market of interested people. I am especially intrigued that most churches don't apply this marketing approach to evangelism, fundraising, and discipleship. It would seem that relationships and influence are their strengths.

Because permission marketing is about the recipients—their needs and wants—many companies and churches choose not to participate. They still want to dominate by initiating conversations and interrupting people with the message of the gospel—or their latest product, program, service, or upcoming event. Also, churches have basically said to the public, "If you want what we have, you are going to have to come where we are at the specific times we are there."

How can you apply permission marketing in your world? What can you do to get your message out to people who are open to hear instead of knocking on doors, making random phone calls, and answering questions no one is asking? This is a challenging question, but it must be answered by every individual and organization in this 21st century world where speed and multiple options rule the day.

Permission marketing has changed my leadership style from one of dominance to one of partnership and cooperation. It has the same potential for you, but the question remains: Do you see the need to change? I guess an even more important and fundamental question is: Do you *want* to change? If you do, what will you do to get the training needed to make and keep those changes? Let's continue our look at permissions marketing in the next essay.

PERMISSION MARKETING 2

As defined in the previous essay, permission marketing is a marketing strategy that emphasizes building relationships with those who want one as opposed to trying to capture those who don't. If you are like me, you get a lot of unwanted mass emails, which are called spam, and circulars in the mail, called bulk or junk mail. Spam is the opposite of permission marketing, for spam sends out thousands or even millions of unwanted and unsolicited emails in the hopes of catching a few people unaware, uninitiated, or vulnerable with messages of why they need what the marketer is selling or peddling. You are annoyed and probably delete spam or better yet, you block it from coming at all. You may even report it to the authorities, since it is actually illegal, but it can be difficult to trace the source.

Why don't more companies and churches employ permission marketing? There are many reasons. One is that they are stuck in the groove of old marketing techniques. *If we can just get our billboard where more people drive,* the reasoning goes, *or if we can write better copy or ads, then more people will buy our product, employ our service, or come to our church.* That may have worked years ago when there was a mass audience and few voices, but in today's world, it doesn't work so well any longer. I have found another reason, a biblical reason, why the old marketing doesn't work and it's pretty simple—because we aren't very good listeners, whether in business or the church, and permission marketing requires that we develop and deploy that skill.

James wrote, "My dear brothers, take note of this: Everyone should be quick to listen, slow to speak and slow to become angry, for man's anger does not bring about the righteous life that God desires" (James 1:19). Being a poor listener is bad for business, whether the business is a church or a company. Yet, we believe if we can just talk to people and get them to hear what we have to say, everything will work out and we will succeed. Actually, the opposite is true: If we learn to listen to others and then shape our messages, products, services, and ministries according to what they want or need, we will succeed. Don't spend time trying to convince people they need what you have. Spend time developing what *they* need and they will beat a path to your door—or church.

I worked with a church one time who bought an elaborate and expensive advertising campaign, complete with TV spots, bulletin inserts, and newspaper advertisements. The program was a colossal failure and they asked me to look at it and tell them what I thought they were doing wrong. After reviewing the program, I couldn't see anything it lacked; it was slick and well done. Then I asked, "Is there anything you do that brings in visitors, the visitors you are trying to get through this ad campaign?" Without hesitation, they answered, "Sure! Whenever we serve food, we get a great response."

Then I asked, "Why don't you serve food?" and they responded, "Because people would only come for the food." I came back with, "Well, what's the difference if they come for food or as a result of an ad?" What's more, when we did the math, we found that feeding people every week for a year would cost half what the ad campaign cost them and would produce twice the desired result, which was new people in attendance. The church, however, wanted to "dominate" the process. They wanted to control what people received (advertising versus food) and they were angry the ad campaign didn't work while the food did. They were so insulted that they refused to feed people, even though they had the money, the cooks, and the facilities to do so.

Companies do the same thing. They want to tell us what we need and not respond to our customer service needs or complaints. Then they get "testy" when we don't respond to their unsolicited interruptions for this or that, or double down to find new ways to sneak their message through to us. Someone once said that we have two ears and one mouth, so we should listen twice as much as we talk. What is your ratio? Someone else said if you are facilitating a meeting and talking more than 25% of the time, you aren't facilitating—you are preaching or teaching. If you lead meetings, what percent is spent in people listening to you as opposed to you listening to them?

I am convinced that the principles and "rules" behind permission marketing are critical for success in the 21st century, no matter what business you are in—including the church. As stated in the last essay, permission marketing takes time and effort, and doesn't happen quickly. Yet if you listen and produce something extraordinary, people will want to hear what you have to say. In today's crowded world of conflicting messages, that is worth its weight in gold.

PERMISSION MARKETING 3

Let's summarize what we have learned so far. The essence of permission marketing is building a relationship with people who *want* to hear what we have to say as opposed to interrupting people with messages they don't want and aren't looking for, using various marketing gimmicks and techniques. I recently went into a sports venue and saw a company's name on the turnstile handles as I went through the ticket gate. That is a perfect example of non-permission marketing. The company thought they had captured my attention and wanted to send a message. They did and the message I heard was, "This is dumb, and I choose to ignore this invasion of my private, mental space." I don't remember the name of the company that put their ads in that conspicuous but ridiculous place.

In the last essay, I mentioned that permission marketing requires listening, while interruptive marketing requires speaking. The latter requires that the company or church initiate and dominate the conversation with the public. Permission marketing requires that the organization listen to the public, something we as humans (even believers) aren't always equipped or willing to do. Listening takes time and turns the conversation the way the listener wants it to go. That is why so many pastors are such poor listeners. They are accustomed to speaking at and to problems and, consequently, they don't really know how to listen. I have seen this to be true the world over.

In the late '80s, Stephen Covey's *The 7 Habits of Highly Effective People* swept the world. I have quoted and taught on his fifth habit many times: *Seek first to understand, then to be understood.* I have learned that when I say to someone, "I know just how you feel. This is my experience in that area," I am actually diminishing their experience and trying to do them one better by telling them my story. For the last two decades, I have worked to ask better questions, listen more intently, give feedback more accurately, and try *not* to speak too soon. I still have a long way to go. Here are a couple of my favorite quotes that have helped me where listening is concerned:

> Listening, coupled with regular periods of reflection, are essential to the growth of the servant leader . . . The most successful servant-leaders are those who have become skilled empathetic listeners." – Robert Greenleaf, *The Power of Servant Leadership*

> Most people do not listen with the intent to understand; they listen with the intent to reply . . . The essence of empathetic listening is not that you agree with someone; it's that you fully, deeply understand that person, emotionally as well as intellectually. – Stephen R. Covey, *The 7 Habits of Highly Effective People*

I have used my weekly *Monday Memo* as an example of permission marketing. I send it only to those who give me permission to do so, and people can easily remove themselves from the mailing list. You may be thinking, "But you, Dr. Stanko, write about what you want to write about every week. Aren't you dominating the conversation?" The answer is that I am, to an extent, but I would not have 12,000 subscribers if

I didn't write about things that were helpful to the reader. If I wasn't a good listener as I travel, teach, and consult, I could not write an effective *Monday Memo*. *The Memo* isn't about me; it's always about the reader—readers who have given me permission to send my material to them because they want to know more about purpose.

So how good of a listener are you? If you don't think it's important, remember what Jesus said: "Therefore consider carefully how you listen. Whoever has will be given more; whoever does not have, even what he thinks he has will be taken from him" (Luke 8:18). If your listening skills are good, then how are you applying them to your work, whether in or out of church? Are you listening to people's needs and working to meet those needs, while still adding to the bottom line (whether that's money, changed lives and communities, or church growth)? That, in my humble opinion, is the essence of permission marketing: listening and serving others' needs.

Eventually, people raise an objection to permission marketing because it draws too much attention to self, whether the self is an individual or an organization—even a church. It has been drummed into believers that they should not, they must not, draw attention to self, for when they do they are glorifying themselves and not the Lord. Let's address that mindset concerning what some consider to be self-promotion in the next Appendix.

APPENDIX THREE

SELF-PROMOTION

One of the common objections I hear concerning the use of social media is that it draws too much attention to one's self. I hear that it is narcissistic and has created a "selfie" culture where people feel the need to broadcast pictures of themselves engaged in various activities or poses. Often, people quote John the Baptist who said, "He must increase, but I must decrease" (John 3:30 NKJV) as a justification for anonymity in ministry and the things of the Lord. That particular verse, however, spoke to their public platform at the time, for Jesus could not take center stage while John held the people's attention.

If anything, if the Church and its members want to exalt their Lord, then it must be more of them so the world can get more of Him. There must be a greater expression and release of the gifts in each individual and the distinctive call and culture of each church, which will require everyone to take their place and manifest His glory. Let's look at a series I have written that spoke to the issue of self-promotion, which is a major concern since it supposedly draws too much attention to the creature instead of the Creator.

★★★★★

SELF-PROMOTION 1

I regularly have discussions with people concerned that they may be promoting themselves rather than the Lord by writing a book or stepping out into other purpose work. They are worried (yes, worried is the correct word) they will get ahead of the Lord, or somehow do something that brings glory to self instead of glory to God. Those are legitimate concerns, but are all based and rooted in fear, and we know God has not given us a spirit of fear. This is an issue I have pondered for a long time, since I have been labeled as self-promoting from time to time, so I am eager to share my thoughts with you as we examine the need to change the way we do church.

CONCEIT

The main objection to self-promotion is best summarized in Philippians 2:3, where Paul wrote: "Do nothing out of selfish ambition or vain conceit. Rather, in humility value others above yourselves." Many conclude talking about oneself in almost any situation is wrong or at least improper, and ambition is also considered to be in bad taste—or downright evil. Are these interpretations correct? Here are some thoughts off the top of my head for this discussion:

1. When Paul wrote his letters, he clearly identified himself as an apostle.

2. David approached Goliath and declared what he was going to do to the giant in no uncertain terms.

3. Jesus made many claims (although sometimes veiled to hide them from unbelievers) concerning who He was and what He had come to do.

Let's examine that last point a little more closely.

A PUBLIC FIGURE

Jesus' family thought he was self-promoting and eager to be a public figure, as we learn in John 7:3-4:

Jesus' brothers said to him, "Leave Galilee and go to Judea, so that your disciples there may see the works you do. No one who wants to become a public figure acts in secret. Since you are doing these things, show yourself to the world."

It's comforting to know Jesus' family thought He was

self-promoting, and to some extent He was—promoting that is, but without being self-centered and with a purpose. Is that possible for us to do the same? If Jesus was misunderstood as He carried out the Father's will for His life, then chances are we will be misunderstood as well.

Weren't Jesus' miracles a means by which He could gather a crowd to announce the coming of His kingdom? Did not the Father make Jesus a household name and a celebrity in all Israel? Did Jesus gather disciples whom He then sent out to extend His work and announce God's plan with even greater intensity and scope than He did?

When Peter and John encountered the disabled man in Acts 3, they ordered him to focus his attention on them: "Peter looked straight at him, as did John. Then Peter said, 'Look at us!' So the man gave them his attention, expecting to get something from them'" (Acts 3:5-6). The apostles didn't insist, "Don't look at us, look at Jesus." They drew the man's attention to themselves, and only then did they give him what God had in store for him through them.

We are not going to settle this issue in this essay, but I wanted to start the dialogue with these thoughts. What do you think? Is it wrong to promote yourself? When, if ever, is it permissible? Does Philippians 2:3 prohibit any kind of ambition or marketing? I leave you to ponder these questions until the next essay.

★★★★★

SELF-PROMOTION 2

We are looking at the propriety and spirituality of being more proactive as we engage in ministry and purpose opportunities. Rather than waiting on the Lord, this life philosophy assumes God is waiting for us to decide where and how we want to be involved in serving Him and others. The basic issue before us is this: What is self-promotion and is it appropriate to engage in it?

YOUR LIGHT

My thought for this essay is found in Matthew 5:14-16, where it says to do your deeds so others can see:

> "You are the light of the world. A town built on a hill cannot be hidden. Neither do people light a lamp and put it under a bowl. Instead they put it on its stand, and it gives light to everyone in the house. In the same way, let your light shine before others, that they may see your good deeds and glorify your Father in heaven."

Later in the same sermon, Jesus gave this warning:

> "Be careful not to practice your righteousness in front of others to be seen by them. If you do, you will have no reward from your Father in heaven. So when you give to the needy, do not announce it with trumpets . . ." (Matthew 6:1-2).

Here we have an important distinction. We are not to parade our righteous acts, such as giving alms, which will glorify self, but we are to show forth our good deeds that will glorify God. Since God has given us our gifts and purpose that will enable us to do your good deeds, I conclude that, in most cases, it is permissible to let people know what we are doing and what we can do when God enables and empowers us to do it.

SERVICE

What's more, if God has given you gifts and a purpose and those are to be used to help others, then isn't letting people know what you can do to serve them consistent with letting your light shine, as we read above? First Peter 4:10 states, "Each of you should use whatever gift you have received to serve others, as faithful stewards of God's grace in its various forms." I can organize and do it quite well since

God helps me do it. Am I ever permitted to say, "I have an organizational gift that is well developed; how can I help you?" It seems adding the thought that my good deeds are to serve others as well as to glorify God makes self-promotion more acceptable and palatable than when it is simply to show off what I can do.

Does this apply to churches and not just individuals? I believe it does. The Church is a city set on a hill. Jesus said no one lights a candle and then puts it under a bushel. If a Church has an effective children's ministry, should it let parents know? Shouldn't that church strive to reach and minister to as many children as it possibly can? Shouldn't that church be willing to train other churches and their workers, sharing what God has shown that church about children? Could that include seminars, books, training videos and other equipping resources? Would it be permissible for that church to purchase advertising in an appropriate medium to announce and promote their children's work so others know what they have? Of course, my answer to all those questions is yes and amen.

When I fly at night and its clear and cloudless, I can see all the cities below the plane. Are they self-promoting? No, they are just doing what cities do at night and that is light the way for their inhabitants to drive, live, and work. They don't build a huge canopy to hide their light because they don't want to attract attention to themselves. Admittedly, it would be strange if those same cities did something to send a message to me in the plane—that would be self-promoting. Otherwise, their light is simply a part of their existence.

The same is true for churches and members. The light they produce cannot help but be noticed and should be used to attract people to the light not only of the gospel, but of the life of the Spirit that is present corporately and individually. Let's move on to the next essay to continue my case for godly promotion of what He is doing in our midst.

★★★★★

SELF-PROMOTION 3

God has assigned you a purpose, made you creative, and given you gifts so you can do His work in creation according to your faith and size of your gift. I recently took a trip to Kenya and took 20 people with me. I am well-known in Kenya where people usually associate me with the purpose message. Kenya represents a place God assigned me to work in accordance with the gifts and purpose He gave me.

I have been on numerous local radio and television shows in Kenya and have spoken in many churches. God opened a door for effective ministry work there, and I have not shrunk back or hesitated to say God sent me there. He put me in the game there, so to speak, and I want to play to the full stature of my abilities and gifts. As I put myself forward in Kenya, I am actually magnifying the Lord, which is the concept I want to discuss in this essay.

MAGNIFY THE LORD

In the Old Testament, we are told to magnify the Lord. We have interpreted that simply as a matter of praise and worship when we exalt and describe God's attributes in clear and perhaps exuberant terms, usually with accompanying music. Yet think about that word *magnify*. Doesn't it also mean to take a small thing and make it larger, so it is easier to see and examine? Could it mean that we are to take the smallest thing God has done through and in us and make it bigger for all to see—not with the intent to see us, but rather seeing us so people can see Him?

I used to see that done in church settings when people gave testimonies, but that is seldom, if ever, done any longer. That is another good reason to use social media, for there we can proclaim His praises through our testimonies for any who are interested to see and learn from (that sounds to me like drawing attention to self in a good way).

Is self-promotion, done with right intent, really any different than giving a testimony? When God does something for you—provides, heals, delivers, reveals, or uses you—is it wrong to stand up and say what He has done—or what you did through His prompting and grace? If God has given you a gift or purpose, is it any different to broadcast the truth of what God has done or can do in and through you? And when you do, is that not the same as magnifying the Lord—taking His work in you and 'blowing it up' for all the world to see?

INTENT

Self-promotion can stem from two sources: the desire to promote ourselves or the desire to further God's work through us as we serve others. Consider what Paul said in Romans 11:13-14: "For I speak to you Gentiles; inasmuch as I am an apostle to the Gentiles, I magnify my ministry, if by any means I may provoke to jealousy those who are my flesh and save some of them" (NKJV).

Paul magnified his office (other translations say "proud of, make as much as I can of, or glorify my ministry") so he could win more people to the gospel. Paul promoted what he did because God appointed him, and that made his work vital. He was not concerned with what others thought, only what God thought. He was telling the truth about himself with the right motives, and therefore he magnified himself so he could ultimately magnify the Lord.

Your job is not just to magnify the Lord by behaving yourself and not robbing banks or watching bad movies. Even heathen can do those things. What they cannot do (but you can) is to manifest God's love for His creation through you, specifically through your purpose, gifts, and goals. Perhaps it is time you realized your distaste for what you call self-promotion is really a means to protect yourself from criticism or being misunderstood. It may also be an attempt to protect your privacy, for once God puts you on "front street," you lose control of your life.

If God wants to put your face on a billboard, it's none of your business. Jesus and Paul 'promoted' and people criticized them; can you expect any different treatment? We will require one more essay to look at this topic and then move on to other topics in this Appendix.

★★★★★

SELF-PROMOTION 4

In this essay, let's finish up our discussion of self-promotion, attempting to define and finalize the definition of what it is and if and when it is appropriate.

TWO THOUGHTS

The two thoughts are really two passages I want us to look at. The first is something Jesus said, which we have looked at in other places in this book:

> "You are the light of the world. A town built on a hill cannot be hidden. Neither do people light a lamp and put it under a bowl. Instead they put it on its stand, and it gives light to everyone in the house. In the same way, let your light shine before others, that they may see your good deeds and glorify your Father in heaven" (Matthew 5:14-16).

Jesus seemed to have no problem with people letting their light shine for the glory of God. That is the challenge, for you may be asking "How do I know if I am glorifying God? What if I am glorifying self?" For that answer, let's go to something Paul wrote as he reflected on people who were self-promoting in the work of the gospel:

> It is true that some preach Christ out of envy and rivalry, but others out of goodwill. The latter do so out of love, knowing that I am put here for the

defense of the gospel. The former preach Christ out of selfish ambition, not sincerely, supposing that they can stir up trouble for me while I am in chains. *But what does it matter? The important thing is that in every way, whether from false motives or true, Christ is preached.* And because of this I rejoice (Philippians 1:15-18a, emphasis added).

It seems Paul did not care about the motives, only that the work of preaching the gospel was being done. Paul was looking at the bottom line or the results, and he was not going to address someone's motives, thus hindering the good work they were doing from the wrong incentive. Others were being helped and it seems God was using the less-than-perfect motives of the worker to get Kingdom results in other people's lives. If that was good enough for Paul, it should be good enough for us.

PEOPLE NEED TO KNOW

You should self-promote not for your benefit but for the benefit of those who are seeking (or who need) who you are, what you have, and what God has empowered you to do. If you can pray and people are healed, then healed people need to know the Lord gave you the gift of healing. If you can write, then let others know you can, for someone reading your book or article may be helped and transformed through your story or ideas.

If you have died in Christ and belong to Him, then your gift, purpose, and role in society are not your choice. If God wants to make you a household name, it's none of your business. There are some members of the body who are created to be behind the scenes, but there are some who are made to be public figures.

On the contrary, those parts of the body that seem to be weaker are indispensable, and the parts that we think are less honorable we treat with special honor. And the parts that are unpresentable are treated with special modesty, while our presentable parts need no special treatment. But God has put the body together, giving greater honor to the parts that lacked it, so that there should be no division in the body, but that its parts should have equal concern for each other (1 Corinthians12:22-25).

Whether you are private or public doesn't make any difference; your life is not your own. It belongs to God and therefore to others. In fact, I would argue that God made some to be in front of an audience, while others to be behind the scenes.

Let's get over any false humility that says, "If God or anyone needs me, they can come find me. I am not going to help them by self-promoting, for that is not spiritual or proper." I say, "Get over it" and let's help all those who need to know and see who we are and what we do to find us more easily and do so without the guilt or feeling of "self-promotion" that can go with that process.

It's time to stand up and say, "This is who I am" whether as individuals or as a church. Will you join me in this thinking, or will you continue to hide your light under a bushel, only then to complain that no one takes you seriously or that God's work is not making progress? If you decide to join me, I promise you will find a new sense of joy and meaning as you trade in your season tickets for a place on the field of play.

APPENDIX FOUR

DEVOTIONALS

I have produced six-year's-worth of daily devotionals that I first published online and then turned into books. Here are three of the thousands I wrote that speak to the issue addressed in Section Three of this book, which is enhanced use of technology and social media for the work of the Church. I include them to show some additional biblical examples of what I believe are instances where the early church and its writers engaged the technology of their day for ministry, and why I believe they would do the same today.

★★★★★

*These devotionals are from my book **The Leadership Walk: Devotions for Leaders of Today and Tomorrow**. With every daily entry, I suggested a leadership step the readers could take as part of their leadership journey.*

★★★★★

1. After this letter has been read to you, see that it is also read in the church of the Laodiceans and that you in turn read the letter from Laodicea - Colossians 4:16.

Paul used the technology of his day—letters and the Roman system of roads and ships—to communicate with his followers and inform them of his latest plans and insights. When he sent this particular letter to Colossae, he made sure they would circulate it among the other local churches. The point is that leaders should use whatever means possible to spread the 'word' to those who need to hear or can benefit from it. If Paul was alive today, he would undoubtedly use all the social media channels to disseminate his message. Modern leaders should do the same.

LEADERSHIP STEP: Are you up to speed on the media available to communicate with those who need or want to hear from you? Stop talking about getting up to speed with the technology and do it. Identify someone to help you and then make time to learn about and register for Twitter, Instagram, LinkedIn, or any other media you could benefit from using. If you already have an account with those social media, then spend your time strategizing how you will use them more effectively.

★★★★★

2. In the first year of Cyrus king of Persia, in order to fulfill the word of the Lord spoken by Jeremiah, the Lord moved the heart of Cyrus king of Persia to make a proclamation throughout his realm and also to put it in writing: "This is what Cyrus king of Persia says: 'The Lord, the God of heaven, has given me all the kingdoms of the earth and he has appointed me to build a temple for him at Jerusalem in Judah'" - Ezra 1:1-3.

Cyrus was king of a sprawling kingdom when the Lord moved on his heart to rebuild the Temple site. The first thing Cyrus did was to communicate his plans throughout his kingdom. How did he do that? He first wrote his plans down and then used the social media and technology of his day to disseminate the information to as many people as possible. Leaders must be committed to broadcast their messages as widely as possible on a regular basis, which means they must be good writers who appreciate and utilize the communication media available to them. That also means leaders must work to stay relevant not only in what they communicate but also in how they communicate it.

LEADERSHIP STEP: Your Step today is to conduct a personal communications audit. How much time do you spend communicating what is most important to you, along with your current insights and ideas? How do you communicate? Do you use the most recent social media? Are you a good writer and speaker or are you working to improve? Do you allow any personal bias to discredit modern technology and its use? Would people say you are an effective communicator?

★★★★★

3. "I have much to write to you, but I do not want to use paper and ink. Instead, I hope to visit you and talk with you face to face, so that our joy may be complete" – 2 John 1:12.

The apostles did not hesitate to use the technology of their day—the Roman road system, waterways, ink, and scrolls—to communicate their teaching and pastoral advice to their flock all over the world. Yet in today's verse, John preferred to communicate through face-to-face encounters as opposed to the written word. Leaders must not only be committed to communicate, they must be willing to use and be proficient in modern technologies. Yet there is still great value in personal meetings, and leaders must not rely too much on technology and eliminate the personal touch that enables them to read body language, tone of voice, and other physical clues and cues from those with whom they are communicating.

LEADERSHIP STEP: Your Step today is to evaluate your use of technology in your communication strategy. Are you confident in your proficiency or do you take pride in your refusal to use it? If you are proficient, are you over-using it to the extent that you neglect or avoid personal contact and face-to-face meetings? Do you have a communications strategy, knowing what you want to share with followers, along with how and when you will share it?

APPENDIX FIVE

THE METRICS OF DISCIPLESHIP

As indicated in chapter eight, believers and churches are expected to bear fruit, however that fruit is defined. I am a proponent of using some type of measurement tool or assessment as a means for corporate or individual spiritual growth. This means you must decide what is truly important—what your fruit should be—and then create some way to measure the fruit of your discipleship efforts, both individually and as a church.

Some people resist any tools that attempt to measure spiritual growth as something foreign to the church and spiritual things, defining them as "worldly wisdom." After all, they ask, how can spiritual matters be measured accurately, and can't the results be used to foster a false sense of spiritual confidence? Their questions are legitimate and their concerns well-founded, for any focus on measuring growth can actually prejudice the measurement itself. This is demonstrated in the parable of the Pharisee and the tax collector:

> To some who were confident of their own righteousness and looked down on everybody else, Jesus told this parable: "Two men went up to the temple to pray, one a Pharisee and the other a tax collector. The Pharisee stood up and prayed about himself: 'God, I thank you that I am not like other

men—robbers, evildoers, adulterers—or even like this tax collector. I fast twice a week and give a tenth of all I get.' "But the tax collector stood at a distance. He would not even look up to heaven, but beat his breast and said, 'God, have mercy on me, a sinner.'"I tell you that this man, rather than the other, went home justified before God. For everyone who exalts himself will be humbled, and he who humbles himself will be exalted" (Luke 18:10-14).

This Pharisee took the evidence or fruit of a life lived for God and made a case for his own righteousness. He was puffed up and proud and missed the more important issue of humility. The Pharisee's blindness and inability to obtain God's perspective as opposed to his own was his undoing. That is the key for any assessment tool or metric for discipleship. In the hands of God, it can be valuable. In the hands of one trying to justify self or someone not interested in spiritual progress, it can provide a false sense of security, dulling the senses and spiritual sensitivities to the Spirit of God. Yet this pitfall need not deter leaders from choosing and then properly and spiritually using and applying tools to help God's people produce what is acceptable and pleasing to Him—both internally and externally.

When we use assessments and measurements and involve God in the interpretation process, those tools can be of great benefit for both individuals and churches. Leaders need not be concerned whether or not God will use these tools. After all, we see God offering an assessment of the churches in the first four chapters of Revelation. He was both ready and able to communicate what He thought of those churches and their leaders.

Can He do that again? Of course, He can. What's more, if the leaders seek the Lord for and understand His evaluation of their work and condition, they will communicate what they have learned to their people and can then apply Spirit-led remedies to Spirit-led growth opportunities. Finally, as individual believers gain an understanding of God's perspective of their own lives and spiritual progress, leaders can assist them by prescribing beneficial programs and initiatives that will unite the people in their individual walk with the Lord, allowing them to progress in holiness and fruitfulness.

Just as He assessed the condition of the churches in the early chapters of Revelation, we see the Lord ready, willing, and able to speak into an individual's life and provide the same kind of assessment on a more intimate basis:

> Now a man came up to Jesus and asked, "Teacher, what good thing must I do to get eternal life?" "Why do you ask me about what is good?" Jesus replied. "There is only One who is good. If you want to enter life, obey the commandments." "Which ones?" the man inquired. Jesus replied, "'Do not murder, do not commit adultery, do not steal, do not give false testimony, honor your father and mother,' and 'love your neighbor as yourself.'" "All these I have kept," the young man said. "What do I still lack?" Jesus answered, "If you want to be perfect, go, sell your possessions and give to the poor, and you will have treasure in heaven. Then come, follow me." When the young man heard this, he went away sad, because he had great wealth (Matthew 19:16-22).

This man came to Jesus for a spiritual assessment of how he was doing, and Jesus let him have it. This indicates Jesus is willing to offer such assessments if we are willing to humbly posture ourselves to receive the results. We must not enter the process with preconceived notions but rather open ourselves, both individually and corporately, to unexpected insights and results that may be both positive and negative as we seek the Lord to ask, "How am I doing?" or "How are we doing?"

Once we have done that, leaders must then help followers understand the implications of God's feedback for their organization, both church and non-profit ministries, and assist individuals as they apply the results to the corporate church setting. In other words, if a church's attendance is shrinking, the leaders must not spin the results, explaining them away to defend their leadership. They must clearly explain the problem and lay out a plan to address it. When leaders do this, the people will be on the same page, and everything done can focus on the common expectation.

In his book, *Technopoly: The Surrender of Culture to Technology*, Neil Postman raised valid concerns that must be considered whenever we embark on the assessment or evaluation process. There are definite limitations and endless opportunities to affect the answers we receive by the questions we ask and how they are worded. Postman's main concern is our inability to be completely objective in our measurement of anything. How a question is worded or presented can make a world of difference in how people respond:

> A question, even of the simplest kind, is not and can never be unbiased ... My purpose is to say that the structure of any question is as devoid of neutrality as is its content. The form of a question may ease our way or pose obstacles. Or, even when slightly altered, it may generate antithetical answers, as in the case of the two priests who, being unsure if it was permissible to smoke and pray at the same time, wrote to the Pope for a definitive answer. One priest phrased the question, "Is it permissible to smoke while praying?" and was told it was not, since prayer should be the focus of one's whole attention; the other priest asked if it is permissible to pray while smoking and was told that it is, since it is always appropriate to pray. The form of a question may even

block us from seeing solutions to problems that become visible through a different question.[1]

Postman's point is well taken and clearly describes the downside of the assessment process. There is, however, an upside that far outweighs it. I am confident that enough good questions can be garnered from Scripture to assist us in the assessment process if we understand the limitations of what we are doing. As Postman warns:

> In a Technopoly, we tend to believe that only through the autonomy of techniques (and machinery) can we achieve our goals . . . We are technical creatures, and through our predilection for and our ability to create techniques we achieve high levels of clarity and efficiency. . . The argument is with the triumph of technique, with techniques that become sanctified and rule out the possibilities of other ones . . . When a method of doing things becomes so deeply associated with an institution that we no longer know which came first—the method or the institution—then it is difficult to change the institution or even to imagine alternative methods for achieving its purposes. And so it is necessary to understand where techniques come from and what they are good for; we must be restored to our sovereignty.[2]

If we are conscious of the limitations of an assessment and open to how God can use it, we, of all people, should be the ones able to keep them in proper perspective. The weakened state of the Church warrants using almost *any* tool leadership deems worthy of helping Christ's body fulfill the Great Commission and be pleasing to God in our corporate and individual lives. The returns will be great for those who work to make their assessment tools a spiritual and not carnal or worldly experience.

Jim Collins made a point in his monograph *Good to Great and the Social Sectors*, with which I fully agree (I have added the emphasis in bold):

> It doesn't really matter whether you can quantify your results. What matters is that you rigorously assemble evidence—quantitative or qualitative—to track your progress. If the evidence is primarily qualitative, think like a trial lawyer assembling the combined body of evidence. If the evidence is primarily quantitative, then think of yourself as a laboratory scientist assembling and assessing the data. **To throw our hands up and say, "But we cannot measure performance in the social sectors the way you can in a business" is simply lack of discipline.** All indicators are flawed, whether qualitative or quantitative. Test scores are flawed, mammograms are flawed, crime data are flawed, customer service data are flawed, patient-outcome data are flawed. **What matters is not finding the perfect indicator, but settling upon a consistent and intelligent method** of assessing your output results, and then tracking your trajectory with rigor. What do you mean by great performance? Have you established a baseline? Are you improving? If not, why not? How can you improve even faster toward your audacious goals?[3]

Are you ready to try to measure your personal or your church's effectiveness? Do you have the courage to measure what is almost impossible to measure? Will you have the courage to face the results whether good or not so good? Can you tolerate others having input into the job you are or are not doing? If so, then go to the next article in this Appendix to read about two measuring instruments and how they can help your church and you.

APPENDIX SIX

SOME
ASSESSMENT TOOLS

In preparation for a school project in my Doctor of Ministry program, I undertook extensive research to identify and understand some of the assessment tools available for use today—both for individuals and churches. I also attended a conference in Florida focusing on the assessment tools from ChurchSmart, a Christian publishing company that produces one particular family of assessment resources. Finally, I completed several of the assessments to evaluate their results and to determine how I could benefit from them as a means to assess and enhance my own spiritual development.

I found every tool I examined could be useful in some way *if* leadership is willing to lead people in how they are to be used and applied. I also found confidence that spiritually mature believers would greatly benefit from using appropriate tools to help assess their current condition and map the way forward to continue their personal development. I will focus on a few tools at this point, not highlighting them as the best that are available, but to help the reader understand how such tools can be used and applied.[4]

1. THREE COLORS

First, let's examine the results of my assessment from Christian Schwarz's book, *The Three Colors of Ministry*.[5] In that book, Schwarz has developed a spiritual gifts profile that not only lists individual gifts, but also divides them into three categories: blue for power or application gifts like faith, prayer, and helps; red for commitment gifts such as giving and hospitality; and green for wisdom gifts such as teaching and administration. When I took the gifts profile, I saw my usual gifts that have previously emerged on similar profiles. With this tool, however, I noticed that all my gifts fell under the red and green categories with none in the blue.

A unique aspect of this profile is Schwarz's belief that he can help the believer identify what he calls "latent gifts." My latent gifts were identified as shepherding, prophecy, wisdom, knowledge, faith, and helps. The latent gifts were obtained from profiles completed by two people who have observed me in ministry situations.

This was just what I needed to see and hear at that point in my life. I had just prior to that accepted a staff position at a local church, which involved curtailing my travels for the duration of the job. These latent gifts were certainly activated, with the Spirit's help, in a local church setting as opposed to my continuing to operate alone away from a local church team. I sought the Lord's direction as to how I could begin to develop and express these latent gifts. Today, during the pandemic of 2020, I have found my fullest and best expression of those gifts through, of all things, social media.

2. THE LIFE PROFILE

Then I took another assessment tool called *The Christian Life Profile Assessment Tool: Discovering the Quality of Your Relationships with God and Others in 30 Key Areas.* This tool has a self-assessment questionnaire along with assessments to be completed and returned by three other people.[6] When I compiled and prayerfully studied the results, this assessment gave me another view of my current walk with the Lord as one of His leaders. What emerged was my "giving away" time, faith, and money were all low. This was quite a surprise for me, since I assumed that these areas were strengths—and perhaps they once were. They had definitely eroded over time, and I made this discovery a matter of prayer and discussion with my spouse.

One tangible act that resulted from this second profile was establishing what I called The Sophia Fund, which I began in Kenya, East Africa. The Fund has served to feed AIDS orphans and widows through the SARAH Network of grassroots organizations working with the poor. I gave the initial donation of five hundred dollars to get this fund started and used my website and other ministry opportunities to raise money for it on an ongoing basis. Since 2009, I have raised hundreds of thousands of dollars, all of which was distributed directly to our Kenyan partners. I have raised money throughout the pandemic for our Kenyan orphans through social media. Speaking of social media, I have found I now give away my time and money in faith through technology.

I don't believe I would have started or even prayed about an undertaking like The Sophia Fund had I not taken to heart the results of this second assessment. This awareness also changed the way I listen and respond to leadership when they talk in church about giving away what I have in my possession to give.

The key to both these profile assessments is I approached them in the fear of the Lord, not looking to justify myself or use my current conditions as an excuse for lack of fruit, but rather to obtain God's perspective on my walk and relationship with Him so I could grow and bear more fruit. This in turn can only make me a better member of my church, for I will not be busy judging the work of the leaders but looking to how I can flow with the Spirit in my local church while walking out God's will for my life.

3. CHURCH PROFILE

Since 1998, I have been certified to administer a church profile called *Natural Church Development* (NCD) that was developed by the aforementioned Christian Schwarz. Schwarz believes he has identified eight key areas essential for church health and growth and has found a way to measure the level and progress of those eight areas in any given church, regardless of theology, mode of worship, or denominational affiliation.[7] The eight key areas are: empowering leadership, gift-oriented ministry, passionate spirituality, effective structures, need-oriented evangelism, loving relationships, inspiring worship service, and holistic small groups.

In the last twenty years, more than thirty thousand churches in the United States, and many more around the world, have taken the NCD profile.[8] According to the statistics, eighty-five percent of those profiled were not growing numerically or spiritually in one or more of the eight areas. This affected church growth in particular, with most not increasing their numbers of those in attendance.

I realize we have not addressed the issue of tracking attendance numbers for church services (a practice to which many are opposed) as a measure of fruit and church health. While I understand their concern, I do not share it. When I was an executive pastor, I never left on Sunday until I had the attendance figures for all three services, along with the same figures for the same Sunday the previous two years. I wanted to know if there was any significant change and then try to ascertain why. If we were not increasing and growing, then how could we justify that in light of the verses that state, "This is good, and pleases God our Savior, who wants all men to be saved and to come to a knowledge of the truth" (1 Timothy 2:3-4)?

If we were not seeing people come to know the Lord or if our attendance was consistently below where it had been in the past, it caused me to go to leadership and pose the question, "Why?" I did not pretend to have the answers, but I knew I had to pose the question and at least try to ascertain what the Lord was saying to us. Let me say that I do not believe attendance figures are the indication of whether a church is healthy or not. Yet attendance figures do tell us something; we must determine, with the Spirit's help, what they reveal.

As reported earlier, of the thirty thousand churches having done an NCD profile, 85% percent showed lack of growth spiritually or numerically in one or more of eight areas. Fifty-four percent of people addressed the lack revealed by the first profile and submitted to a second follow-up profile within twelve months of the first one. The second profile showed that 46%, or 13,770 churches of the base of thirty thousand had improved in the area with the lowest score and had also grown numerically since the first profile. Even if a church is growing numerically, it should determine whether or not this increase is from new believers, from people who left and have returned to church, or from those who have simply transferred from another church.

The whole philosophy of the NCD profile is one that can only help improve leadership communication in any congregation. After the profile is administered, the strategy is to identify one of the eight characteristics with the lowest score, called the minimum factor. Then leadership develops a strategy to improve in that one area and that one area alone. This simplifies and streamlines the communication process from leadership, which allows members to put aside their opinions and ensure everyone in the church is pulling together in the same direction.

Once a second profile is completed (usually one year after the first), the church can identify another minimum factor, which would then be addressed by leaders and members alike. The process can go on as long as the local church senses the results are spiritual and relevant. There are some churches that have used the profile annually for ten years, and the results are consistent: there is growth, the church is united in direction, and the leadership and members always know the current emphasis for church growth and development. Such is the power of a spiritually developed and applied assessment tool.

DRAWBACKS AND CONCERNS

A concern may be raised that these profiles are technical and non-spiritual, as mentioned earlier. I would argue the opposite. The NCD church profile is simple and involves church strategies in aspects of church and community life that violate no biblical principles. What could possibly be wrong with a church addressing their deficiency in need-oriented evangelism? What is the harm in any church working to improve the loving relationships among members? What could possibly be the damage done as members identify their spiritual gifts and determine, with leadership's assistance, how those individual gifts can be expressed in the local church and beyond?

As long as the leaders and members seek to apply the results with the Spirit's help, I fail to see how this process cannot do anything but help the local church. The worst that can happen is the leadership or members reject the results of the profile as inconsequential under the Spirit's leading. The best that can happen is there will be a consistent definition of fruit, thus releasing the John 15 principle of believers bearing unlimited fruit in the will of God. Another possible benefit is the people of God moving in one direction as a congregation.

If a spirit of humility is employed as members and leaders seek to address their current status, the assessments can be used by God to direct and guide. I recommend that each one apply the lesson from the following parable as he or she approaches any assessment tool:

Suppose one of you had a servant plowing or

looking after the sheep. Would he say to the servant when he comes in from the field, "Come along now and sit down to eat"? Would he not rather say, "Prepare my supper, get yourself ready and wait on me while I eat and drink; after that you may eat and drink"? Would he thank the servant because he did what he was told to do? So you also, when you have done everything you were told to do, should say, "We are unworthy servants; we have only done our duty" (Luke 17:7-10).

The goal is not anyone feeling smug about his or her spiritual condition or progress when the assessment is done. While there may be cause for rejoicing that God's grace has allowed for some spiritual growth and fruit, the measuring tools should always be used to address deficiencies so the believer and the church can be growing and making progress in the will of God.

This essay is not written with the intent of defending or selling any one profile or assessment tool. It is presented in the hope that these tools will be seen as possible aids to enhance leadership communication and member involvement in local church efforts. As mentioned in the previous essay, Collins wrote that what we do in non-profits (and churches) is almost impossible to measure. That, however, does not exempt us from trying to measure and assess our growth and progress.

IN CONCLUSION

Without some tools enabling us to assess our spiritual state, whether individually or corporately, we are doomed to repeat the same mistakes according to the same limited knowledge and understanding that has restricted or hindered our walk or progress in the Lord up to that point. Our growth will be limited and not as rapid as when we use a tool that posed spiritual questions so we can obtain spiritual answers previously not seen. To obtain conclusions with which we can disagree is a better situation than to be left with each person offering their suggestions and opinions for their own spiritual state or the condition of their local church.

Let us not shy away from our attempts to measure spiritual growth and to identify the metrics of discipleship. I firmly believe as we seek to apply the results from any assessment, the Lord will help us to uncover and identify blind spots and areas of great opportunity to know Him better and to become more like Him. From there, our fruit will only be limited by our faith, God's gifting, and His purpose for each life.

APPENDIX SEVEN

A BIBLICAL VIEW
OF GROWTH
AND INCREASE

The Bible consistently talks about increase in the life of the individual and in the life of the church. Yet how can we measure that growth? And in what areas do we seek to do so? Those are the challenges for the individual and leaders as they seek to "continue to work out [their] salvation with fear and trembling, for it is God who works in [them] to will and to act according to his good purpose" (Philippians 2:12-13). We discussed these issues in the previous two essays. Let's look at one parable and then list some other verses for you to consider on your own. The parable is from Matthew's gospel:

> Again, it will be like a man going on a journey, who called his servants and entrusted his property to them. To one he gave five talents of money, to another two talents, and to another one talent, each according to his ability. Then he went on his journey. The man who had received the five talents went at once and put his money to work and gained five more. So also, the one with the two talents gained two more. But the man who had received the one talent went off, dug a hole in the ground and hid his master's money.

After a long time the master of those servants returned and settled accounts with them. The man who had received the five talents brought the other five. "Master," he said, "you entrusted me with five talents. See, I have gained five more."

His master replied, "Well done, good and faithful servant! You have been faithful with a few things; I will put you in charge of many things. Come and share your master's happiness!" The man with the two talents also came. "Master," he said, "you entrusted me with two talents; see, I have gained two more."

His master replied, "Well done, good and faithful servant! You have been faithful with a few things; I will put you in charge of many things. Come and share your master's happiness!"

Then the man who had received the one talent came. "Master," he said, "I knew that you are a hard man, harvesting where you have not sown and gathering where you have not scattered seed. So I was afraid and went out and hid your talent in the ground. See, here is what belongs to you."

His master replied, "You wicked, lazy servant! So you knew that I harvest where I have not sown and gather where I have not scattered seed? Well then, you should have put my money on deposit with the bankers, so that when I returned I would have received it back with interest. Take the talent from him and give it to the one who has the ten talents. For everyone who has will be given more, and he will have an abundance. Whoever does not have, even what he has will be taken from him. And throw that worthless servant outside, into the darkness, where there will be weeping and gnashing of teeth" (Matthew 25:14-30).

A parable is a story containing a moral or lesson. We must be careful not to overanalyze the details in any parable, unless Jesus Himself explained them, as He did in the parable of the prodigal son and the parable of the sower. In the case of this parable in Matthew 25, the focus isn't on the number of talents, the master, or the servants. The lesson is simple: God expects increase. How much increase? It doesn't seem to matter. He just expects increase. The one who was fearful and did not show any increase was condemned. You should not evaluate this story on whether or not the judgment on the non-producer is fair. It is a story with an exaggerated emphasis so the lesson will stand out: God wants increase.

Below are some other biblical exhortations that speak of increase and growth in our walk with the Lord and one another. The question isn't whether or not we should increase and grow but rather how can we know whether or not we are doing so. What are the acceptable metrics of our discipleship and church work? Hopefully, you can use these verses for your own personal study or to lead others into a better understanding of just how important increase and fruit is from God's perspective.

- And this is my prayer: that your love may abound more and more in knowledge and depth of insight, so that you may be able to discern what is best and may be pure and blameless until the day of Christ, filled with the fruit of righteousness that comes through Jesus Christ—to the glory and praise of God (Philippians 1:9-11).

- And God is able to make all grace abound to you, so that in all things at all times, having all that you need, you will abound in every good work (2 Corinthians 9:8).

- And we pray this in order that you may live a life

worthy of the Lord and may please him in every way: bearing fruit in every good work, growing in the knowledge of God, being strengthened with all power according to his glorious might so that you may have great endurance and patience, and joyfully giving thanks to the Father, who has qualified you to share in the inheritance of the saints in the kingdom of light (Colossians 1:10-12).

- So neither he who plants nor he who waters is anything, but only God, who makes things grow (1 Corinthians 3:7).

- Neither do we go beyond our limits by boasting of work done by others. Our hope is that, as your faith continues to grow, our area of activity among you will greatly expand, so that we can preach the gospel in the regions beyond you. For we do not want to boast about work already done in another man's territory (2 Corinthians 10:15-16).

- But grow in the grace and knowledge of our Lord and Savior Jesus Christ. To him be glory both now and forever! Amen (2 Peter 3:18).

- Finally, brothers, we instructed you how to live in order to please God, as in fact you are living. Now we ask you and urge you in the Lord Jesus to do this more and more (1 Thessalonians 4:1).

- And in fact, you do love all the brothers throughout Macedonia. Yet we urge you, brothers, to do so more and more (1 Thessalonians 4:10).

- We ought always to thank God for you, brothers, and rightly so, because your faith is growing more and more, and the love every one of you has for each other is increasing (2 Thessalonians 1:13).

"'Take the talent from him and give it to the one who has the ten talents. For everyone who has will be given more, and he will have an abundance. Whoever does not have, even what he has will be taken from him. And throw that worthless servant outside, into the darkness, where there will be weeping and gnashing of teeth'" (Matthew 25:28-30). (*The lesson of this parable is that God expects increase, not maintenance of the status quo.*)

- And the Lord added to their number daily those who were being saved (Acts 2:47).

- No one else dared join them, even though they were highly regarded by the people. Nevertheless, more and more men and women believed in the Lord and were added to their number (Acts 5:13-14).

- So the word of God spread. The number of disciples in Jerusalem increased rapidly, and a large number of priests became obedient to the faith (Acts 6:7).

- For this very reason, make every effort to add to your faith goodness; and to goodness, knowledge; and to knowledge, self-control; and to self-control, perseverance; and to perseverance, godliness; and to godliness, brotherly kindness; and to brotherly kindness, love. For if you possess these qualities in increasing measure, they will keep you from being ineffective and unproductive in your knowledge of our Lord Jesus Christ (2 Peter 1:5-8).

These verses prove beyond any reasonable doubt that God requires and expects increase and growth in every area of life, work, and ministry.

NOTES FOR
APPENDICES

[1] Neil Postman, *Technopoly: The Surrender of Culture to Technology*, 1992, Vintage Books, NY, 125-126.

[2] *Ibid.*, pages 142-143.

[3] Jim Collins, *Good to Great and the Social Sectors: A Monograph to Accompany Good to Great,* published by Jim Collins, 2005, pages 7-8.

[4] I have administered a number of profiles in church settings and have found them invaluable as they provide a common language for members and workers to understand one another and to appreciate the God-given differences from one believer to another. They include The Leadership Circle 360 degree feedback profile, the Personality Profile involving the DISC, TEAMS, and VALUES profiles, the *Birkman Profile,* and one called *Your Leadership Grip.*

[5] Christian Schwarz, *The 3 Colors of Ministry: A Trinitarian Approach to Identifying and Developing Your Spiritual Gifts,* ChurchSmart Resources: St. Charles, IL, 65-86.

[6] Randy Frazee, *The Christian Life Profile Assessment Tool Workbook: Discovering the Quality of Your Relationships with God and Others in 30 Key Areas,* Zondervan: Grand Rapids, Michigan, 2006, 32-43.

[7] Christian Schwarz, *Natural Church Development: A Guide to Eight Essential Qualities of Healthy Churches,* ChurchSmart Resources: St. Charles, IL 2006, 18-48.

[8] *Ibid.*, page 7.

ABOUT THE AUTHOR

John Stanko was born in Pittsburgh, Pennsylvania. After graduating from St. Basil's Prep School in Stamford, Connecticut, he attended Duquesne University where he received his bachelor's and master's degrees in economics in 1972 and 1974 respectively.

Since then, John has served as an administrator, teacher, consultant, author, and pastor in his professional career. He holds a second master's degree in pastoral ministries, and earned his doctorate in pastoral ministries from Liberty Theological Seminary in Houston, Texas in 1995. He recently completed a second doctor of ministry degree at Reformed Presbyterian Theological Seminary in Pittsburgh.

John has taught extensively on the topics of time management, life purpose and organization, and has conducted leadership and purpose training sessions throughout the United States and in 32 countries. He is also certified to administer the DISC and other related personality assessments as well as the Natural Church Development profile for churches. In 2006, he earned the privilege to facilitate for The Pacific Institute of Seattle, a leadership and personal development program, and for The Leadership Circle, a provider of cultural and executive 360-degree profiles. He has authored fifteen books and written for many publications around the world.

John founded a personal and leadership development company, called PurposeQuest, in 2001 and today travels the world to speak, consult and inspire leaders and people everywhere. From 2001-2008, he spent six months a year in Africa and still enjoys visiting and working on that continent, while teaching for Geneva College's Masters of Organizational Leadership and the Center for Urban Biblical Ministry in his hometown of Pittsburgh, Pennsylvania. John has been married for 44 years to Kathryn Scimone Stanko, and they have two adult children and two grandchildren. In 2009, John was appointed the administrative pastor for discipleship at Allegheny Center Alliance Church on the North Side of Pittsburgh where he served for five years. Most recently, John founded Urban Press, a publishing service designed to tell stories of the city, from the city, and to the city.

KEEP IN TOUCH WITH JOHN W. STANKO

www.purposequest.com
www.johnstanko.us
www.stankobiblestudy.com
www.stankomondaymemo.com

or via email at johnstanko@gmail.com

John also does extensive relief and community development
work in Kenya.
You can see some of his projects at
www.purposequest.com/contributions

PurposeQuest International
PO Box 8882
Pittsburgh, PA 15221-0882

ADDITIONAL TITLES BY
JOHN W. STANKO

A Daily Dose of Proverbs
A Daily Taste of Proverbs
Changing the Way We Do Church
I Wrote This Book on Purpose
Life Is A Gold Mine: Can You Dig It?
Strictly Business
The Faith Files, Volume 1
The Faith Files, Volume 2
The Faith Files, Volume 3
The Leadership Walk
The Price of Leadership
Unlocking the Power of Your Creativity
Unlocking the Power of Your Productivity
Unlocking the Power of Your Purpose
Unlocking the Power of You
What Would Jesus Ask You Today?
Your Life Matters

Live the Word Commentary: Matthew
Live the Word Commentary: Mark
Live the Word Commentary: Luke
Live the Word Commentary: John
Live the Word Commentary: Acts
Live the Word Commentary: Romans
Live the Word Commentary: 1 & 2 Corinthians
Live the Word Commentary: Galatians, Ephesians, Philippians,
Colossians, Philemon
Live the Word Commentary: Hebrews
Live the Word Commentary: Revelation

Made in the USA
Coppell, TX
29 September 2021